yakuza moon

yakuza moon
memoirs of a gangster's daughter

Shoko Tendo

Translated by Louise Heal

KODANSHA INTERNATIONAL
Tokyo · New York · London

This translation is based on the Japanese version of the book published by Gentosha, Tokyo, in 2006, under the title *Yakuzana Tsuki*. Originally published by Bungeisha, Tokyo, in 2004, under the title *Yakuzana Tsuki*.

Distributed in the United States by Kodansha America, Inc., and in the United Kingdom and continental Europe by Kodansha Europe Ltd.

Published by Kodansha International Ltd., 17–14, Otowa 1-chome, Bunkyo-ku, Tokyo 112–8652, and Kodansha America, Inc.

First edition, 2007
15 14 13 12 11 10 09 08 07   10 9 8 7 6 5 4 3 2

Library of Congress Cataloging-in-Publication Data
Tendo, Shoko, 1968-
  Yakuza moon : memoirs of a gangster's daughter / Shoko Tendo ;
translated by Louise Heal. -- 1st ed.
    p. cm.
  ISBN 978-4-7700-3042-9
  1. Tendo, Shoko, 1968- 2. Yakuza--Japan. 3. Gangs--Japan--Biography.
  4. Children of gangsters--Japan--Biography. 5. Organized crime--Japan.
  I. Title.
  HV6439.J3T46 2007
  364.1092--dc22
  [B]
                                        2006039555

www.kodansha-intl.com

Contents

CHAPTER ONE

Floating Clouds

I was born in the winter of 1968, a yakuza's daughter. I was the third child of four born to my father Hiroyasu and mother Satomi. My brother Daiki was twelve years older, and then came my sister Maki, just two years older than me. Finally there was Natsuki, five years younger than me and the baby of the family. We always called her Na-chan.

We originally lived in Toyonaka, in the north of Osaka, but when I was very young, we moved to a brand new house in Sakai on the other side of the city. It was a beautiful house, guarded by double iron gates. Beyond was a winding stone path lined with pink and white azalea bushes that led up to the front door. The house itself was large by Japanese standards—each of us had our own bedroom, and there was also a living room, a dining room, two Japanese-style tatami rooms, and one room where my father ran his business and met with visitors. I remember that the whole house was filled with the scent of fresh timber. Our sitting room looked out onto a large pond in the style of a castle moat, with multicolored koi carp that glided gracefully through the water. We even had a swimming pool where we played all day long throughout the summer. Right outside my bedroom window was a tall flowering cherry tree, which was a kind of friend to me. Whenever I had worries or problems, I used to go and sit under its branches.

Besides being the boss of the local yakuza gang, my dad managed three other businesses: a civil engineering company, a construction firm, and a real estate business. To all of us kids, he was a larger-than-life character. His obsession was cars, and he always owned several brand new models, both Japanese and foreign made, not to mention all the Harleys and other motorcycles. Our garage looked like a car showroom with its perfect array of gleaming polished cars and motorcycles. Of course, he was never satisfied with the basic versions and used to spend his spare time souping them up. If someone else in a hot rod pulled up next to him at a red light, he would rev his engine like a drag racer then floor it the moment the light turned green. My dad at the steering wheel was the stereotypical duck to water. My long-suffering mom would beg him not to drive so fast, but I always got a huge kick from the sensation of speeding.

Every weekend my family would go out together shopping or to a restaurant. Whenever we left the house, Dad's crocodile skin wallet would bulge as if it had just swallowed a very large prey. Mom would always sit in front of her three-sided mirror to perform the ritual fixing of her hair and meticulous application of makeup. She'd step out clutching a pale pink parasol in her delicate white fingers. I'd hold her other hand and stare at her opal ring that reflected the sunlight in a rainbow of colors. "When you're grown up this will be yours," she'd say, looking down at me with a smile.

Dad was extremely busy running his gang and his other businesses, but he would always spend the first week of the New Year with the family. We couldn't wait to dig into my mother's traditional homemade feast: vegetables simmered in soy sauce, thick slices of sweetened omelet, sugared black beans, golden chestnuts steamed with rice, all arranged on three tiers of black lacquerware. On New Year's Day, after we'd eaten, the family would go out to the nearby shrine and say the first prayer of the New Year. We kids would pick a fortune scroll and have our parents read and explain it to us. This was a Tendo family annual ritual. My first New Year's after starting school, Dad came up to me and placed a talisman in the shape of a tiny bell into the palm of my hand.

"This is for you, Shoko."

That talisman felt so warm there in my hand, as if its power reached into the depths of my being. I hung it on my school satchel, and at recess would finger it and listen to the tinkling sound of the little bell, lost in happy New Year's memories.

My parents were always kind, but they were strict about manners. Even our housekeeper was told not to spoil us, and we were never allowed to watch television while eating. We had to give thanks before and after meals, and when we were done, we always had to clear away our own plates. We were brought up the old-fashioned way, but I liked it.

Our home was always filled with the lively comings and goings of car salesmen, jewelers, kimono salesmen, tailors, and all sorts of people. It was a fascinating world for a little kid to grow up in.

My grandpa on my dad's side doted on me the most of all his grandchildren. One day, when I was three years old, he was bouncing me on his knee singing, "Shoko, Shoko," and just like that fell asleep. It turned out he had died of a heart attack. Four years later, soon after I started elementary school, my grandma also passed away. After her funeral, we were sitting down to lunch when one of my uncles came over to my father.

"You yakuza scum. You're not getting a penny of the Tendo family's money," he spat.

"The funeral's not even over yet and you're already talking about the money? Fuck off and leave me alone, you bunch of vultures!" my dad roared, and stormed out.

The rest of my relatives sat there with their eyes on the floor. I felt sick that these people could pick a fight about money when my grandma had just died. I remember thinking that Dad might be a yakuza, but this time he was definitely in the right.

A few days later, Dad got into some trouble and was put in jail. We'd never had much to do with our neighbors since moving to the area, but suddenly everyone seemed to be gossiping about us—and all of it was nasty. It was my first experience of discrimination, but it wouldn't be my last.

Once, when I was drawing a picture in front of the house, one of the women in our street came over. She bent down and whispered in my ear, "Shoko-chan, did you know that your big brother isn't your real brother? Your mom had him before she met your dad."

What she said didn't have any effect on how I felt about my brother, but I couldn't understand why someone would tell a child something like that. And the neighborhood children quickly picked up on their parents' attitudes. At school, I was called "the yakuza kid" and treated as an outcast. My elementary school years turned into six years of constant bullying.

There was something that happened when I was in second grade that I'll never forget. It was cleaning time, and it was my group's turn to clean the teachers' room. I was down on my hands and knees wiping the floor, so I was hidden between two desks. When I heard the familiar voice of a teacher who was always kind to me, I pricked up my ears.

"Shoko Tendo? She can draw, and maybe her basic reading and writing's OK, but that's about it. There's not much you can teach an idiot like that."

She sounded disgusted and I saw her toss a sheet of paper onto her desk. The other teachers gathered around to look.

"You're not kidding!" they laughed.

It was my recently graded test paper. I might not have done very well on the test, but I'd tried my hardest. Then they caught sight of me standing there stunned, and hurriedly said, "Is the cleaning done? Good job!" With false smiles plastered on their faces, they ushered me out of the teacher's room.

That was how I learned that people can be two-faced, a lesson I never forgot.

In those days, children between the ages of four and fourteen weren't allowed to visit prisons, so Maki and I never had the chance to meet or talk to our dad. Mom had taken over the running of the businesses, as well as the job of watching over the younger gang members. She was forced to take baby Na-chan along with her everywhere, but she just got on with it, quietly waiting for the day when Dad would be released. I never heard her complain once. Still, I didn't want to cause her any more worry, so I never mentioned what went on at school.

But then, because I didn't tell anyone about it, the bullying quickly became a daily routine. My gym clothes and sneakers were dumped in the furnace, and on cleaning duty I was always the one who had to scrub the floors. Most of the time I was so totally ignored that it felt like I didn't exist. The kids who were responsible for most of the bullying and prejudice were mainly those with the best grades and parents in elite jobs. Their methods of bullying were so sly and ingenious that unless I made a fuss, the teachers never noticed. I knew there was no point telling anyone; it would only make things worse. The bullies would just try all the harder not to be caught next time. But no matter what they dished out, I never cried or skipped school unless I was really sick.

My only friends were my notebook and pencil. I spent recess and lunch hour drawing pictures, ignoring the taunts of my classmates.

"Your dad's a yakuza. Scary!"

"Guess your dad won't be coming to parents' day, seeing as he's in jail!"

"What's wrong with being a yakuza?" I'd shoot back, because the only thing I couldn't stand was my parents being insulted. And even though being a yakuza's daughter meant I was treated like dirt, I decided I wasn't going to pretend to be something I wasn't, just to make friends.

When I got home from that hateful place, our dog and cat were always waiting for me at the front door. I'd sit and stroke their soft fur and I'd feel calmer. Human beings lie and do cruel things, but animals are different. The koi I fed every day would hear my footsteps and follow me around the pond. They needed me, and to me they were more than just pets, they were members of our family. When I looked out of my bedroom window in spring, I could see petals of cherry blossom dancing in the spring breeze like snowflakes, and my heart would dance along. If I put my ear gently to the tree trunk, I was sure I could hear a tiny pulse beating, and I felt as if the tree was talking to me. When summer came and the cherry had lost all its blossom, I would lie under it, watching the sky and picturing the world beyond the floating clouds. When I was little, home was the only place I could ever be really happy.

Mom was very special to me. I was quite a sickly child, and so she was always worrying about me and was never far from my side. But this also meant I was constantly scared that she would disappear from my life. One time when I was sick in bed, I opened my eyes and found Mom wasn't there. I tried calling her, but she didn't answer. I ran out into the street in my bare feet to look for her. Eventually I met her on her way back from the store.

"What are you doing? You're supposed to be in bed," she said, with a puzzled look on her face.

I couldn't explain why I had been so scared. While I was sick, Mom would bring me meals in bed—rice porridge with a bright red pickled plum on top, and shiny yellow half-moon peaches. I can still remember the faintly sweet taste of the porridge and the tang of the salty plum. I couldn't have known how short lived these tender moments spent with Mom would be.

I was home from school with a fever one day, when Mizuguchi, one of the younger yakuza in my dad's gang, slipped into my room. He came over to where I was lying on the futon.

"Are you feeling sick, honey?"

There was an unusual gleam in his eyes, and I sensed something strange about the way he was acting.

"Yes," I answered, doing my best not to look at him.

"Shoko-chan, you're such a big girl now, and you're getting prettier all the time."

Mizuguchi brought his face up close to mine and tried to kiss me. I struggled as he stuck a rough hand inside my pajamas and grabbed my breast. I could see the tattoo on his arm peeking out from underneath his shirt cuff. Somehow I managed to kick and punch my way out of his grasp, but I was so terrified my whole body was shaking and I almost threw up. A few days later, Mizuguchi was arrested on a drug charge.

I could never really trust adults after that.

Soon after I started fourth grade, Dad was released from jail. He began to go out every evening to expensive bars and come home in the middle of the night with bar hostesses on his arm. He'd yell, "Satomi! Shoko! I've got a present for you. Come and help me eat it." I didn't want to get my dad mad when he'd been drinking, so no matter how sleepy I was or how full my stomach, I'd leap out of bed.

"Looks yummy, Dad."

And I'd force a smile as I finished every last bite of the cakes or cookies he'd brought home. It was around this time that I started to put on a lot of weight. At school the bullying got worse, and I was called things like "pig" or "blimp."

I hated seeing my dad come home drunk every night. Or rather, I was disgusted by the hostesses, stinking of perfume, with their sickly sweet voices.

"Here we are now. Home safe and sound!"

They'd be draped all over him, right in front of Mom and me. Even then I was smart enough to see that they didn't give a damn about my dad; they were after his money. I felt terrible for Mom as she bowed her head to these women and thanked them politely for their help.

Whenever Dad was in a bad mood, he would roar at the top of his lungs and take it out on everything in the house. Thickset and muscular, once he went on a rampage, he wouldn't be able to stop himself. He'd break windows or rev the accelerator of a brand new car until it blew the engine. I can't even count the number of times we had to replace a television set or telephone. Na-chan, the youngest, would get into my futon and cling to me, terrified.

"Shoko, I'm scared, I'm scared."

"Na-chan, go back to sleep. Nothing bad's going to happen to you while I'm here."

I pretended to be the tough older sister, but I was quaking inside. Then, when everything had finally quieted down, I would get up and help Mom clear up the mess. She'd be crying as usual.

"Don't worry about me," she'd say, "You've got school tomorrow. Go back to bed."

But I didn't want to leave her, so I pretended not to hear and kept on picking up.

"When I grow up, I'm going to be rich and buy a new house for us to live in," I'd say, trying to cheer her up.

The next day, Dad would be amazed at the state of the house.

"What the hell's been going on here?" he'd ask.

He'd have no memory whatsoever of his rage and that is why, although I feared him, I could never bring myself to hate him.

There was a period when Dad became so busy with his yakuza-related business that he was almost never at home. The people who worked in his home office were often out too, so I found myself alone in the house a lot. The phone used to ring incessantly, and when I answered, a voice would say something like, "After three o'clock tomorrow this check will be dishonored. Please make sure you tell your parents right away. Don't forget, OK?"

The caller would hang up, but the word "dishonored" left a nasty aftertaste. Although I didn't understand what it meant, I could tell that something bad was happening. Dad began to pore over his blueprints late into the night, meticulously remeasuring and redrawing lines. Sometimes he would just sit at his desk for hours with his head in his hands.

I knew that Dad worked as hard as he could to support us, but when I crawled into my futon at the end of the day, all I could think about was how he was going to come home drunk and trash the place again. I'd stare up in the darkness of my room at the grain in the wood of the ceiling, and after a time it would begin to look like a creepy face and I'd turn rigid with fear. When Mom came to bed, I'd sneak a look at her face as she slept on the futon next to mine. Only then would my body relax and I'd be able to close my eyes. Those days I never got a good night's sleep and found it impossible to concentrate at school. To tell the truth, I was never into schoolwork in the first place, so sleepy or not, I don't suppose I would have studied much anyway.

And then, after six painful years, my elementary school education finally came to an end.

CHAPTER TWO

Cheap Thrills

Around the same time I finally graduated from elementary school, my older sister Maki began to cut school and became a *yanki,* one of those wild kids who bleach their hair and race around in illegal hot rods or on motorcycles without mufflers. She dressed in flashy clothes and looked way older than a middle school student. Of course, I thought she was totally cool. But this hero-worship was about to turn my life upside down.

It was the spring before I started middle school. Late one night, I happened to catch Maki as she was about to sneak out of the house. Afraid that I might rat her out, she asked me if I wanted to come along. I felt guilty when I thought of Mom, who was already worried sick about Maki's behavior. I knew it'd be hard on her if another of her daughters became a yanki too. But I was dying to find out what Maki was up to.

Maki used her artistic talent to swiftly transform me from a twelve-year-old girl into a precocious teenager, plastering my face with thick makeup and dressing me up in some of her loudest clothes. I felt like a real yanki as we got into the taxi and headed downtown. Outside the taxi window, the streets were jammed with garishly painted hot rods, and gangs of yanki kids hung out on every street corner. It just wasn't the same place as in the daytime—night had turned the city into a yanki paradise, lit by tacky neon lights. The atmosphere buzzed with excitement.

Maki paid the fare and the taxi door opened. Frigid night air flooded in around our feet. Trying to shake off the chill, we hurried as fast as our high-heeled shoes would take us toward a sign that said *Minami Disco*. "If anyone asks how old you are, say you're eighteen," warned Maki, before we got into the elevator. By the entrance, there was a large sign that read OVER 18 ONLY. I began to panic. I didn't look eighteen. There was no way I'd get in.

Maki rolled her eyes at me, and pushed me through the door. She held out the entrance fee in a very womanly hand tipped with red-painted nails. Getting in was so easy it was a total anticlimax.

I stepped onto the dimly lit dance floor and was almost knocked off my feet by a huge wave of sound. The bass rhythm of Earth, Wind and Fire's *Boogie Wonderland* felt like a rumbling from the earth that vibrated up through my feet and spread through my whole body. Looking around, I realized the sign at the door should have read YANKIS ONLY. Although it was early spring, the room was as hot and steamy as if it was the middle of summer. In bizarre contrast to the heat and the noise and the heaving crowd of people dancing like demented maniacs, a mirror ball turned slowly overhead, casting beautiful rainbow lights over the scene.

As I stood there gaping like an idiot and feeling totally out of place, an older yanki-looking girl came up to me.

"Hey, how old are you?"

She obviously wasn't one of the staff, so I broke the promise I had only just made to my sister.

"I'm twelve."

"Seriously? I thought you were about the same as me. Come over here and meet the gang."

She dragged me by the hand to a nearby table and sat me down. Maki was already having a blast with her friends on the dance floor and was paying no attention to me.

"Hey, hey, how old do you think this girl is?" the yanki girl asked the guy who was sitting next to me. He'd shaved his hairline back into a deep V-shape over each temple, the better to show off his bad-boy pompadour hairstyle.

"About seventeen?"

"Way off. She's only fuckin' twelve."

Everyone at the table turned and stared at me.

"No shit? What's your name?"

"Who are you here with?"

Suddenly everyone wanted to know about me.

"I'm Shoko. I came with my sister, Maki."

"No shit! You're Maki's little sister..." The shaved-headed guy leaned closer and looked me up and down. I wasn't sure if he was satisfied by my response or if he was just carried away by the beat of the music, but he nodded his head as he spoke. The yanki girl introduced herself.

"Yeah, Maki and me we're good buddies. My name's Sayuri. Hi."

She passed me a glass of ginger ale, and everyone shouted out *kanpai!* and clinked glasses. I felt like I'd died and gone to heaven. I had friends for the first time in my life. It seemed yankis were OK people after all.

"Shoko, get your butt over here!" yelled Sayuri from the dance floor as Wild Cherry's *Play That Funky Music* thumped from the speakers. We danced until closing time.

It was almost dawn as we got a ride home from one of Maki's friends in his shocking-pink Nissan Skyline. The car rode so low to the ground my butt was bounced around all over the place, but I felt as if I was floating on air. Saki Kubota's *Ihojin* blared out of the car stereo. It was the big hit song at the time and it had been played to death, but right then it seemed fresh and new to me. Back at the house, the two of us crept through the yard and climbed through Maki's bedroom window. We changed into pajamas, hurriedly took off our makeup, and collapsed onto Maki's futon. But I was too pumped to sleep. It was the first time I'd ever done anything like this.

From that day on, I was a yanki.

When I started middle school a month later, I had already pierced my ears with a sewing machine needle heated up in the flame of a cigarette lighter and dipped in antiseptic. I wore full makeup, painted my nails, and dressed like a typical yanki. But I still went to school every day. Looking like this, nobody dared to say anything to me and the bullying stopped completely.

One day, however, my homeroom teacher summoned me to the teachers' room.

"Tendo, get that hair fixed!" she bawled.

"Why should I? It's naturally this color."

"Liar! Until you dye it black again there's no way you're coming into my classroom."

At these words, all the pent-up anger I felt against teachers exploded.

"What did you say? Who the fuck do you think you're talking to?"

With that, I shoved the whole contents of the teacher's desk onto the floor, then kicked her chair as hard as I could. She certainly didn't expect a response like that, because her tone quickly changed from a hysterical screech to a saccharine attempt to calm me down.

"I'm afraid it's just against school rules."

Then, looking as if she was about to wet herself, she got rid of me as quickly as possible.

Asshole.

I didn't go back to my classroom and I didn't go home either that day.

This was the first of many times that I would run away from home. By the end of the day, everyone in the school had heard what had happened, and I was branded a yanki for good.

Instead of going home, I went to Natsuko's place—she was one of the older girls in my gang—and I told her the whole story.

"That really pisses me off. That's why I hate teachers." Natsuko spewed this out along with her cigarette smoke. She was a hardcore yanki. She'd been going to school until recently, but had had a huge argument with some teacher or other and quit going completely.

"Right, we're going to be buddies," she announced, and after bleaching her own hair used the rest to turn mine platinum blonde. She lent me some clothes, and we rode around sitting with our butts half out of car windows, sniffing paint thinner and laughing like crazy late into the night.

I never even called home after that, spending nights at different gang members' homes. I started dating Yuya, who was two years older than me. People had been telling us we'd make a good couple, and so it seemed like we might as well get together.

All the other girls in the gang had long since lost their virginity. Like them, I had never taken the idea of sex very seriously—to us it was just a kind of rite of passage to becoming an "adult." I was in such a hurry to seem grown up that when Yuya asked me to go to bed with him I went—clutching a bag of thinner in one hand. Yuya slept around quite a bit, and it was obvious that he wasn't serious about me, but as it was my first time, I didn't really care. I figured someone like Yuya would do just fine.

Yuya slipped off my clothes like he'd done it a million times before and made to kiss me. Suddenly that horrible memory from my childhood snuck into my head. His hand moved down from my breast, and now I had no doubt what was going to happen. He opened the drawer of the bedside table and produced a box of condoms. He turned his back to me as he put one on...

"Does that hurt?" he asked.

"No," I replied, but actually it was very painful.

When it was finally over, the sheets were stained with blood. I was scared that this was going to give away that I was a virgin, so I deliberately spilled some thinner and pulled off the sheets, balled them up, and shoved them in the washing machine. Still, Yuya went around informing his friends that it had been my first time, and worse, that I'd had no reaction when he touched me—I was totally frigid. Yuya's words hurt me, but they were particularly painful because they happened to be true. Sex with him hadn't been the least bit pleasurable.

It may have been the stress or being strung out on thinner most of the time, but somehow, without realizing it, I lost a huge amount of weight. Occasionally I would go back home, only to be confronted by Dad in a total fury, yelling things like, "What the hell have you done to your hair?" He'd grab the nearest object—an ashtray or something—and bash me over the head with it. He'd keep on hitting me as hard as he could until I thought I was going to die. But I would never apologize or go to see a doctor. I'd just go and lie down and rest until I felt better. Sometimes my mother would try to put herself between us. The sight of this tiny woman, her hair all messed up, begging me to stop getting into trouble and Dad to stop hitting me, was far worse than any physical pain. I hated making her cry like this, but it did nothing to curb my appetite for playing around.

Maki had also fallen into the pattern of running away from home, being found, dragged back, and beaten up by Dad. She would wait for her wounds to heal and then be off again—the typical yanki lifestyle. But after being picked up by the police a few times, she was held in a detention center. She was released once on probation, but because she refused to change her lifestyle in any way, she was sent back again.

She ended up in a juvenile prison. Shortly after she was sentenced, I heard from my friends that Yuya was also in juvie. Since that time we'd had sex, we hadn't even spoken, so I couldn't have cared less.

Every night I hung around downtown or rode around in hot rods. I'd never had a bad trip yet from thinner, and did some every day. My crowd of friends kept on growing.

When I was in eighth grade, a friend of mine called Makoto, a guy three years older who was a in a motorcycle gang, introduced me to a girl the same age as me. Yoshimi and I soon started to hang out all the time. One day, we got a summons from some of the older girls in our gang who thought we were getting too cocky. When we got to the place, we realized we were in trouble—there were four girls and two guys lying in wait for us. We knew we had no chance of winning, but if we could beat up even one of them it'd be worth it, so we went for it. The result was predictable—Yoshimi and I were beaten to a pulp.

After they left, we dragged ourselves back onto our feet. Yoshimi produced a battered pack of Seven Stars from her pocket and handed me a cigarette.

"Thanks."

I stuck it in my mouth and blood began to soak into the filter. Yoshimi offered me a roaring flame from her ¥100 lighter, almost setting fire to my bangs.

"Hey, Shoko. You wanna get revenge?"

"You bet. You?"

"Next time we'll really fuck them up!"

Yoshimi was seriously pissed off. Her cigarette shook in her hand.

"Let's go to Makoto's place," I said, as I knocked the dust off Yoshimi's clothes for her.

"Right. I want enough thinner to get totally wasted."

The two of us got on a motor scooter with no muffler that Makoto had stolen and customized for us a few days before, and headed off to his place.

Several days later, I was summoned by a different girl. This time three girls and a bunch of guys were waiting for me.

"Shoko, what the fuck is that skirt?" And without warning, she smashed a liter-sized bottle of thinner into my head at the same time as her foot slammed into my stomach. As I crumpled, holding my belly, my head was pinned to the ground by a dirty old shoe.

"Get on your knees and apologize!" she shouted. She began to kick me frenziedly.

"No way!" I leapt to my feet, and punched her full in the face.

"Rape her!" she screamed at the four waiting guys, and immediately one of them came up and took hold of me by the hair. He dragged me to his car and pushed me into the back seat. As Quincy Jones' *Ai no corrida* blared out of the speakers, he climbed on top of me. His breath stank of thinner.

"Hey, you, hold her legs down for me!" he yelled at one of his fellow gang members.

"No one's gonna rape me. Get the fuck off!"

I kicked him in the balls as hard as I could and tried to climb out of the car, but he grabbed at my clothes and I fell headfirst onto the asphalt. One of the guys, Tomonori, who was in my grade at school, couldn't stand to watch this anymore. He caught my would-be rapist by the arm.

"Stop it. Let her go."

"Get your hands off me, scum. Who the fuck do you think you're talking to?" Infuriated, the guy threw Tomonori to the ground.

"I've had enough of being told what to do by assholes like you," Tomonori yelled back, getting to his feet and bursting a bag of thinner in the guy's face.

"Aagh!" He fell to the ground with his hands over his eyes.

"Shoko, get on!"

I scrambled onto the back of Tomonori's metallic pink Honda CBX 400, fashionably customized with the high handlebars that were all the rage at that time, and with the seat cushions removed to make the seat lower. Looking at Tomonori's hand on the grip, it was hard to believe he had anything in common with the guy who had just tried to rape me.

"Are they behind us? Can you see?" Tomonori called back to me. I peered over my shoulder.

"No, I can't see them."

"There's no way a Skyline could ever catch me on this baby."

"You're gonna be in the shit after this..."

"It's worse for you."

"Whatever. I don't care," I said, trying to sound more laid-back than I felt.

"Me neither. Just because they're older doesn't mean they can treat us like shit, right?"

"Yeah."

I really didn't care about the fight. After all, it wasn't the first time the older gang members had summoned me and it probably wouldn't be the last, either. So I couldn't figure out why I was trembling. Then I realized. That horrible voice was in my head whispering, "Shoko-chan, you're such a big girl now..."

Despite all that had happened, I didn't make any changes to my life-style. I still hung out with friends, and from time to time, if the mood took me, I went to school. Well, more accurately, as my hair and uniform were worn in a style that completely broke school regulations, I just went to visit the teachers. As soon as they caught sight of me, the other students would look disgusted. It might have been partly due to the red, swollen eczema that had appeared on my inner arm, on full display in my short-sleeved uniform, but they all looked at me as if I was something dirty. The only reason I bothered to show my face there at all was because of the school counselor, one of the few people who cared enough to chew me out. He even used to hit me sometimes, but at least he was different from most of the other teachers, who pretended I didn't exist. He had a conservative attitude, but I felt there was something very human about him. By getting to know him, I was managing to overcome my own prejudices against teachers. Although he was young, my homeroom teacher was also doing all he could to deal with my problems, and the principal too was a tolerant man. Having learned that there was in fact such a thing as a good teacher, I went to the teachers' room in search of my seventh-grade homeroom teacher, the one I had lost my temper with that time in the teachers' room.

"Sensei, I'm sorry about that other time…" I said, hanging my head.

"Tendo-san, I think I said some bad things too. Why don't you come back to my classes? I'll be expecting you," she replied, and even smiled.

The whole thing was really embarrassing, but somehow I felt relieved that I had apologized.

But by the time I reached ninth grade, I was still running away from home and had stopped going to school altogether. I used to have fun hanging out with Yoshimi and her gang. We were heavily into sleeping pills, which we would crush between our teeth and then wash down with soda because we thought this would make them work faster. Then we'd fight off sleep by sniffing thinner, and enjoy the buzz it gave us.

Once, Yoshimi and I happened to wake up at the same time. The TV had been left on and a news program was just starting. We turned and stared at each other in amazement, then rushed to the mailbox to get the newspaper.

"Shoko, this is bad. Looks like we've been asleep for three days."

"Like a pair of real-life Rip van Winkles."

We burst out laughing.

So most of the time we did dumb stuff like this and laughed about it. But once, after I'd taken a huge dose of the sleeping drug Benzalin, I was so spaced out that when one of the guys in the gang—someone I didn't like much—climbed on top of me, there was nothing I could do to stop him having sex with me. When I woke up the next day with my head on his shoulder, it came back to me what he'd done, and I had to run to the bathroom to puke my guts out.

I started smoking marijuana too, and not a single day passed without getting high. Everyone referred to marijuana by innocuous terms like "grass," "weed," or "hashish," so I never thought of it as anything more than "naughty tobacco." Some kids quickly moved on from this to speed. There were girls around me who took up prostitution to feed their habit, and I saw how they would sleep with anyone to get their hands on some speed. There was always someone around offering me a fix, but I was never tempted. I never wanted to end up like them.

Around this time, a bunch of us were hanging out in front of a game arcade one afternoon, when I heard someone shout, "Hey, you! Shoko! You're giving the boss a lot of grief."

I looked around to see one of the yakuza from Dad's gang, a man called Kobayashi. Everybody flung away their hidden bags of thinner and scattered in all directions like baby spiders. It wouldn't matter whether it was the middle of downtown or anywhere else, if Kobayashi caught us, he would make us all kneel down and listen to his lecture, delivered with a face like some fierce gargoyle. If I dared to take an attitude, he'd slap me and drag me home, and this time Dad would probably beat me to death. I didn't have the strength left to go through all that again.

"Hey, come back here!"

Kobayashi had abandoned his Toyota Crown and was chasing us on foot. We had the edge on him until we found ourselves trapped on the fourth floor of an office building, with nowhere left to go. There was nothing for it but to jump from a window onto the roof of the next building, and continue running.

"Shoko, I can't believe that old fart's climbing out after us."

"What's he thinking? If he falls he won't be able to beat us up anymore!"

"Wish he would."

Kobayashi was in good shape, but we could see he was pretty much out of breath. But then again, we'd been doing thinner, so we were about to drop too.

"Kobayashi can't still be following us."

"Yeah, gargoyle-face is right behind us."

"Shit!"

"No. I'm kidding. He's not there. He's not there."

"It's no time for jokes. If he catches us he's gonna kill us this time."

"Yeah, we really are running for our lives."

We collapsed laughing.

In fact, although he disapproved of my wild lifestyle, Dad had actually told Kobayashi to leave me alone. But for some reason Kobayashi had taken it into his head to try and hunt me down. Like I didn't already have my hands full running away from the police.

"Shit, I'm bored. I hate this rain."

It was Rie who spoke, sitting propped up against a wall sporting a poster of a gang of kittens dressed up in yanki gear. It was an eighties obsession to own one of these posters. The cats were known as the *nameneko*, and there was a whole series of posters featuring them dressed in different outfits. It had been raining nonstop for several days, and we had been holed up in one of our regular hideouts, strung out on thinner. This was how we got through the monotony of the rainy season.

"At least it's going to be summer vacation soon. We can get the older guys to drive us to the beach and stuff."

"Yeah, it'll be a blast."

"With luck there'll be some cute guys this time. Hey, anybody wanna go buy some peroxide? Do some highlights?"

"Cool."

Putting peroxide in our hair was about the high point of our day. We couldn't wait for vacation to begin. Unfortunately, this year, summer would turn out to be anything but fun...

The rainy season was barely over, and we were still living the everyday humdrum life of the yanki when Yoshimi got mixed up again with the same girl we'd been in trouble with that time back in the eighth grade, and was summoned to meet her.

"I could go on my own, but I'm sure there'll be a bunch of them waiting," she said, doing her best tough-girl impression. I decided to go with her to the hangout. As we'd guessed, there were four girls waiting for us. It turned into a huge free-for-all, and soon the police showed up. We were arrested on charges of inflicting bodily injury, then handcuffed, roped around the waist, and hauled off to a waiting patrol car.

"Dumb-ass kid. Get in the car now!" said one of the officers. He kicked me in the back then smacked me over the head. I took off the cuffs, which were on so loosely there was no point in even using them, and threw them in his face.

After we got to the police station, I refused to sign a confession. The officer from the juvenile division was so frustrated by my attitude that he kicked me in the shins under the interview room table, banged his fist repeatedly on the tabletop, and finally upended the whole thing. I was determined not to let him get to me, and the interview ended without me so much as opening my mouth. The officer gave up and wrote the charge sheet.

"Sign here!" he said, thrusting the paper under my nose. I didn't react. No matter how many times he told me, I just sat there.

"I see you're that mob leader's daughter. Like father like daughter. The phrase really applies in this case. You've certainly got balls."

I thought it was ironic that as soon as he realized the interview was going nowhere, he brought up the subject of my father. I wasn't that tough. I just knew that whatever I said I was only going to incriminate myself further. That and the fact that the police had found ordinary aspirins in my bag and labeled me "in possession of drugs." The police are very practiced at trumping up charges. A few days later, I was moved to a temporary detention center, next door to Osaka Prison.

Most days at the detention center were spent reading or making collages. We rarely had the opportunity to get any exercise so I looked forward to the couple of times a week that we were allowed to play table tennis. I was in solitary confinement but I could hear faint laughter percolating through from the communal cell next door. Although the new arrivals usually hated solitary confinement, I didn't mind it too much, and I was comfortable being by myself. When you got used to it, you felt quite free. Food was doled out from an oversized cooking pot, but for some reason, the miso soup was brought in a blue plastic container that strongly resembled a garbage pail. A tray was then pushed through a hatch in the wall of the cell. The soup had barely any ingredients added to it and tasted watery, but the rice was mixed with barley, and it tasted pretty good. From next door, I could hear someone on the verge of tears complain, "The rice is disgusting. I can't eat this crap." I realized that some of the girls were really miserable, and I felt bad for them. The summer weather had finally kicked in, and when the lights went out at night, the place was as hot as a steam bath. It was impossible to fall asleep right away. In the middle of the night, I could hear the roar of motorcycles belonging to some gang or other piercing the silence, reminding me that I was no longer free. It was salt in the wound. I couldn't believe I was spending my summer in a place like this. It felt like a long time ago that we had all had fun hanging out together. Even the moon seemed to tease me. Its rays shone right into my face as I tried to peer out of the window, yet it stayed far from my grasp, on the other side of the bars. How could something that felt so close be so out of reach?

I heard the jangling of keys as the guard approached.

"Tendo, you've got a visitor."

The lock creaked and the heavy iron door swung open. It was the first time I had been taken to the interview room, and I followed the guard with some trepidation, my eyes firmly on my own feet. I wondered how many yankis had walked this exact same route before me.

The door opened and there sat a little old lady I'd never set eyes on before, holding a can of Coke. It turned out to be my ninth-grade home-room teacher. Seeing as I hadn't set foot in school since moving up to ninth grade, it wasn't surprising we'd never met. Yet she'd bothered to come visit and brought me a gift.

"Tendo-san, please stop making such trouble. You should try to turn over a new leaf." Her voice trembled slightly when she spoke.

"Yeah...well, uh, thanks for the Coke."

And that was the end of my conversation with the only person who ever came to visit me.

Later that day, one of the guards handed me a book. It was a collection of poems, including traditional haiku and tanka poetry, written by inmates from all the girls' correctional facilities in the country. The authors were identified by their initials. One girl had been awarded the top prize in all three categories: freestyle poetry, haiku, and tanka. This previously-unheard-of triple-crown win had gone to none other than my own sister, Maki.

> On the proud bloom of our youth
> Please bestow sanctuary and light
> Like a warm and gentle breeze
> That travels o'er fields of green
> And the clear blue ocean

> Reading her letter
> I can feel my mother's warmth
> Fill my empty heart

> Far away from me
> My dear father and mother
> I offer to you
> My deepest apologies
> With truly heartfelt sorrow

I couldn't control my laughter any longer. As I rolled around on the tatami floor in hysterics, I thought of how Maki had been beaten up time after time, and kept running away from home over and over again, never sorry about a thing. "Truly heartfelt sorrow…" Yeah, right. And the irony that an older sister could compose poetry in juvie that her younger sister would find herself reading in a detention center—I just had to laugh.

"Tendo! What's so funny?" came the reproving voice of a guard, but the more I tried to control myself, the harder the laughter came. I laughed so much my stomach hurt.

A few days after that, I met my parents for the first time in a very long time—in the family court. The interior of the courtroom was oppressively silent, as though everyone was waiting with bated breath for judgment to be pronounced on me. Sitting in the back of the room were two people I'd never seen before, and I quickly realized they were guards from either a reform school or a juvenile prison. The judge gave my address, name, age, and then began to read the list of charges.

"Shoko Tendo. While missing from home, inhaled paint thinner, and perpetrated an assault. Of the victims, three sustained injury. The accused was also found to be in possession of drugs. She has refused to make a voluntary confession, so this court is unable to determine whether she feels any remorse over her actions."

At the time of my arrest my parents hadn't reported me missing, so the term "missing from home" was inaccurate. When I was arrested, I had no thinner on me. I would have to be caught red-handed with the thinner or have confessed to inhaling it in order for that to be used as evidence. On top of that, my over-the-counter aspirins were being classified as drugs.

"Shoko Tendo, do you have anything to say?"

I knew a denial would be pointless. I shook my head.

The judge adjusted his glasses, and turned to my parents.

"Would the parents of the accused care to make a statement?"

"Nothing but a deflated ball, that one," offered my dad.

The judge had never heard a father reply like this before.

"A deflated ball?" he parroted.

"Yes. It doesn't matter how much her parents worry about her. She's like a deflated ball—if you try to throw it, it will never fly straight and it will never bounce back. She has to take responsibility for her own actions. Otherwise she's never going to become a better person."

Dad's words were as harsh as I'd expected. I gave them a sideways glance and noticed that my mother was wiping tears from her eyes.

"Shoko Tendo, please take note of what your father has said. I'm sentencing you to a reform school."

The two guards behind me had apparently been waiting for this moment and now they approached me. "Let's go," they said, gently steering me away. At that moment, I heard my mother's voice.

"Shoko-chan!" She squeezed my hand.

"I'm sorry I've caused you so much trouble," I said. "I'll see you."

I was too upset to squeeze her back, and as I gently tried to extricate myself from my mother's grip, I felt her tear fall onto the back of my hand.

"Be strong," added Dad, looking me straight in the eyes. Then the guards led me out into an empty corridor. The only sound was the lazy slap of worn-out rubber-soled slippers on the polished floor. I left the courthouse without even glancing back.

As soon as I arrived at the reform school, I was taken to a room where a folding chair had been placed in the middle of the floor.

"Sit here. I'm going to cut your hair," said one of the teachers, indicating the chair.

She ruthlessly chopped away at those highlights I was so fond of. I could only watch as my hair fell onto the sheets of newspaper spread around my feet. I was forced to listen to an explanation of the rules through the chopping noise of the scissors. When she had finished, I quickly brushed away the hair that had fallen in my lap and changed into the burgundy-colored jumpsuit that was to be my uniform.

The regimented days at reform school were the polar opposite of my old lifestyle. Each morning began with roll call. Then we'd wash briefly and do our chores. Next we'd prepare and eat breakfast, clear it away, and then it was time for lessons. These included embroidery and needlepoint, which I couldn't stand. There was also some simple farm work—

spreading manure and stuff. Phys. ed. was mostly running, but I wasn't very strong and found it hard to run long distances. (Although I could run forever when I knew a cop or Kobayashi was behind me . . .) But there was no point in making excuses here. All the rules were geared to living a group lifestyle, and there was no choice but to fit in. For someone like me, who had always done exactly as she liked, this was a valuable learning experience. It was only through having my freedom taken away from me that I truly began to understand its importance. I knew what Dad had said that day in the courtroom was true. You have to take responsibility for your own actions. You do bad stuff and this is what happens. I was the only one involved in that fight who had ended up in a reform school, but that was OK. If they'd just released me from the detention center, I wouldn't have gone home—I'd have gone straight back to my friends and our hangouts. It was surely only a matter of time before I ended up in here anyway.

Although I was quite sincere in my self-reflection, I also managed to get into trouble. I'd been born with hair that was naturally brown rather than black, but when some peroxide disappeared from the medicine box, I was the one blamed.

"You've used it to bleach your hair!" screamed the teacher.

I was reminded of that time back in seventh grade when I was attacked by the homeroom teacher over my hair color, and I lost my temper.

"Look! This is my own color," I yelled back, and pulling out a handful of my own hair by the roots, I threw it in her face. Then I pushed her as hard as I could and ran for it. I managed to dodge all the teachers who came after me, and headed for the fence. The school relied on our consciences more than physical barriers to stop us escaping—the fence wasn't very high. I felt bad about it, but I wasn't going to put up with being accused of something when I was innocent. I headed for Hiromi's place. She was one of the older girls in the gang and she happened to live close by. We spent about a week lying around getting wasted on thinner until finally she'd had enough.

"Shoko, you'd better go back to the school," she said. "If you keep this up, next time you'll end up in juvie. Anyway, you can't stay with me forever. And you've nowhere else to go. No one's going to want to get mixed up with a runaway."

Hiromi had even pawned some of her parents' possessions to make sure I had money, and now she handed me my taxi fare. It was true what she said—my other friends had been afraid that if I was taken back to the reform school they would be picked up too, so they'd all been avoiding me. This girl was the only one who'd looked after me. She'd had to persuade the guy she lived with to hide me in their home. The truth was, she had spent some time in juvie herself and knew how tough it was in there. That's why I decided to take her advice and returned to the reform school of my own free will. The staff asked me repeatedly where I'd been and what I'd been doing, but I never let on. As punishment I was forced to stare at a wall and meditate from morning to night for a whole week, breaking only for meals. During this time I often used to think about the teardrop that my mother had let fall on my hand in the courtroom, and the sorrow my parents must have felt as they watched me being taken away. I understood the pain I'd caused to everyone, but I still hadn't learned my lesson.

One morning eight months later, I was told that I'd be released the next day. That night I couldn't sleep at all. I just lay there waiting for the light to start filtering through the curtain. When daylight finally came, I leapt up, opened the window, and took a long, deep breath of cool morning air. I answered the final roll call, changed from pajamas to uniform, and ate breakfast there for the last time. After gathering up my belongings, I went to the tiny hall where all of us who were leaving were presented with our middle school graduation certificates by the principal of the reform school. My parents had come to collect me, and they watched all this silently from the back of the room. The moment the leaving ceremony was over, I ran over to them.

"Let's go home," said Dad with a smile, patting me on the shoulder.

"Yeah."

Dad's hand on my shoulder was warmer than the spring sun, and my mother was even laughing. We got in the car, and I waved good-bye to the teachers who had been my surrogate family for the past eight months. The city didn't seem to have changed much, and it looked wonderful under the cloudless spring sky.

We had just reached our house and got out of the car, when I heard someone call my name. I looked up and there was Yoshimi, tottering toward me in a pair of gold sandals with four-inch heels. As usual, it looked like she was on Benzalin or something.

"It's *so* good to see you. I missed you, girl!"

I don't know if it was fate or what, but we spoke the same words at the same time. We hugged, and I was really happy to see her.

"I heard from Maki that you were getting out today, so I thought I'd come and meet you. Everyone's dying to see you. Come on."

Yoshimi was tugging on my hand. My parents had already gone into the house, leaving the front door open for me. They stood in the entranceway, saying nothing, but their eyes pleaded with me to follow them. As I turned away without even setting foot in my family home, I felt my parents' eyes bore into my back. My heart did feel heavy, but I wasn't yet grown up enough to resist the allure of a good time.

The hangout turned out to be the same old cluttered room, where there was barely room to walk. The same old faces were there, with the same old bags of thinner.

"Hey, Shoko! We've missed you! How was it in there?"

Osamu grinned as he passed me the plastic bag, displaying his missing front tooth, the result of doing too much thinner.

"It was fucking boring. I couldn't stand it."

"You haven't changed a bit, same old Shoko! But now for some serious partying!" Osamu hooted with laughter. It felt like I'd never been away—everyone was exactly the same. The eight months I'd been shut away in a reform school felt like some sort of dream.

The next day, reeking of thinner, I went to visit the school counselor from when I was in eighth grade. He smiled when he saw me.

"It's nice to see you again, Tendo. Are you going to be taking things seriously from now on?" he asked, taking my arm.

"I don't know about that. I just wanted to see you, Sensei."

"If you're not going to sort out your life now, then what's going to become of you?"

"I'd like to change, but I can't make any promises."

"Hmm. Well, at least you're honest."

"I can't lie to you, Sensei."

"So you can't even say you'll make an effort?" he asked, his tone turning serious.

"I'm not sure I've got it in me."

"Then what on earth was the point of spending eight months in a reform school? Was it a total waste of time?"

"No, I learned a lot. Thank you, Sensei."

Perhaps I'd had some kind of romantic image of myself as the reformed delinquent coming back to thank the one teacher who had cared enough to chew me out. But this wasn't a movie.

"Come and see me again anytime," he said, patting my shoulder.

"Yeah...sure, I guess...," I mumbled, embarrassed.

Outside the school gates, Kosuke revved the engine loudly.

"Kosuke, sorry!"

As I climbed onto his metallic purple Kawasaki FX, Kosuke sounded the horn. It was customized to play the intro to *The Godfather* at top volume.

No, I hadn't changed a bit, but little did I know that big changes were ahead for my family.

CHAPTER THREE

Speed

Our family's bad reputation ruined my brother's marriage plans. His fiancée's parents decided to look into our family background. When they came to explain to my parents why they wouldn't allow their daughter to marry Daiki, they made their feelings quite clear.

"Two of his sisters have been in prison or reform school. It's not really acceptable." Of course, they wouldn't have had the balls to say, "His father is a yakuza. Sorry." But the fact that his sisters were both juvenile delinquents was probably the nail in the coffin for that relationship. I felt lousy for what I had done to my serious, hardworking brother.

"It's not your fault," said Daiki. "It just wasn't meant to be. Anyone who can turn me down for a reason like that isn't the person I'd want to spend the rest of my life with anyway."

But I knew we'd screwed things up for him.

A mean rumor began to go around that the reason Daiki was still single was that there was something "wrong" with him. Where do people get off nosing around other people's affairs and starting rumors? We were brother and sister, but we were two completely different people. Why did anyone need to lump us together?

I felt bad, but I never for one second thought about giving up my wild lifestyle.

That summer, Dad suddenly fell seriously ill with tuberculosis. He hovered on the border between life and death, and then somehow pulled through, but even when he got his color back and started to walk again, the big, burly gang leader had become a scrawny little man. My mother was busy caring for Na-chan, who was still just a kid, as well as running Dad's businesses in his absence. Maki had recently got married and gone to live with her husband's family. There was no one else to care for him, so I was the one who spent the next few months nursing him back to health.

Of course I was still a yanki, and at the age when I wanted to be out having a good time. It sucked not being able to hang out with my friends, but hoping that somehow I could help speed up Dad's recovery, I stuck it out and never left his side.

But there were other problems. Dad was in a private room in the hospital, which was a lot more expensive than a regular bed. If he needed anything, I had to go and buy it at the hospital store, which charged outrageously high prices, so it really started to add up. Our family was already in financial difficulties by this time, so money was a real worry.

Every day a little old lady called Fujisawa-san, one of Dad's fellow patients, would come to his room for a visit. She had been an invalid since she was young and had spent most of her life in hospitals, but she always managed to stay cheerful. She was also very curious about the outside world, and extremely polite.

"And what is your name, young lady?" she asked in her melodious birdsong voice, the first time I met her.

"My name's Shoko."

"Really? May I call you Shoko-chan?"

"That'd be fine."

"Shoko-chan, your hair is a beautiful color. Would you mind if I touched it?"

"Go ahead."

"I've never felt blond hair before. It's so soft—just like a doll's." She gave a delicate laugh.

Fujisawa-san was the first adult who had spoken to me without judging me by my appearance. Chatting to this old lady as we strolled through the tiny area of green in the hospital grounds was calming to my soul. The air smelt fresh, and if I breathed deeply it felt as if my lungs, habitually filled with cigarette smoke, were being purified.

Sometimes I would sketch the plants and flowers. I didn't pick them because I didn't feel they would want to be placed in a tiny vase and have people admire them. Here in this garden they weren't ever going to catch many people's eye, but I felt that they would much prefer to die in the place they had lived. I'm sure it was Fujisawa-san's kindness that made me begin to think this way. She would encourage my father to write haiku poetry, and she even entered one into a competition organized by her haiku club. And he actually won a prize. I realized that Maki's triple-crown win had been because she took after her father. From that time on, Dad became fascinated with haiku. Fujisawa-san's encouragement truly helped him through his sickness and took his mind off his money problems.

One day I went to buy a can of soda from the vending machine and noticed a wallet lying on the floor nearby. I checked the contents and found a large wad of cash: ¥180,000. When I was a kid, my parents used to give me pocket money to buy cute pencils and stuff for school, but for obvious reasons, since I became a yanki they'd stopped giving me anything. I never had money for clothes, so Maki and I used to share the few we had. Among my friends, there were girls whose parents bought them cars, clothes, makeup, and even gave them spending money on top of that. So to me this was a huge sum of money, and of course I wanted to keep it, but I felt that somewhere God was watching me, so I handed it in to the nurses' station. Right after that, as I was sitting with Dad in the cafeteria, there was an announcement over the hospital loudspeaker announcing that some lost property had been found next to the vending machines. A little later, a nurse approached us pushing a wheelchair. In it sat a man in pajamas, about the same age as Dad. The man looked amazed to see that a yanki like me had handed in a wallet containing that much money.

"So you were the one who found my wallet. I don't know how to thank you." He really did look relieved. He reached into his wallet and pulled out ¥20,000. "Here. It's not very much, I'm afraid..."

"Are you a patient here?" I asked, not taking the money.

"Yes. My son brought me this money yesterday when he visited. I must have dropped it when I was buying a drink. I'm really grateful to you."

"You don't need to give me money. Please just get well soon."

"But I insist."

"No, I don't want to take it."

"That's right," Dad added, for support. "It's enough for us to see you have a speedy recovery."

"Well, thank you. You've got a good daughter there. I hope you get to go home soon, too."

The man bowed deeply and then left the cafeteria, wheeled away by the nurse. His words had left me feeling embarrassed, but secretly pleased. At just sixteen, I felt very far from a "good daughter."

"Dad, I never told the nurses my name," I said later that evening as I sat by his bed. "How did they know how to find me?"

"You're the only one around here dressed like some kind of clown."

"Oh..."

"By the way, what made you decide to hand the wallet in?"

"Well, I did want to keep the money, but I thought if the owner was someone like you, y'know, who was a patient here, then it'd be a real bummer to lose it. Anyway, it turned out he was, so I'm glad I was honest."

"I see... That's what it was. You did a good thing."

He smiled and stroked my head affectionately. I couldn't remember when I'd last seen Dad smile like that. He definitely never complimented me or stroked my head... Had we sat and had a conversation like this even once since I'd been a yanki?

Out of the window I could see the night sky. The stars were usually fairly hazy, but tonight the air was clear and they twinkled brightly. I remembered when I was a little girl and my family used to go to visit one of Dad's friends in the countryside near Nara. We'd look up at the night sky and if we spotted a shooting star, we'd make a wish, hurrying to say it three times before the star disappeared. There was a little river with rushes on the bottom that waved in the current. On summer nights, fireflies would flit around it, giving off their pale light. I used to only have to call this scene to mind to relive the magic of those evenings. But now I realized that I couldn't hear the murmur of the stream anymore. It was as if its banks had been concreted over and the fireflies had died out. At some point, Dad's thoughts had flowed eastward and mine westward, leaving nothing but a dried-up riverbed. But somehow that night our minds had merged once again. I felt close to Dad for the first time in a long while.

Unfortunately, that feeling of happiness would be as fleeting as a shooting star.

Dad had been the guarantor for an acquaintance's loan, but the man suddenly skipped town, leaving huge debts. Dad desperately tried to pay the loan off, but business was bad and he was forced to turn to all kinds of shady moneylenders. Before he knew it, his companies were just scraping by day to day. As the debts mounted up, things started to spiral out of control. It became impossible for the companies to be run without Dad there on the spot, but he was still in the hospital. He had permission to leave once or twice a month, but could only spend a few hours at home in that time. Before long, he retired from the yakuza. I imagine he no longer had the strength—physically, financially, or mentally—to carry on the lifestyle.

Our family was now plunged into debtor's hell. The interest on our loans was going through the roof. The loan sharks would charge an increase of 10 percent every ten days, then it would jump to 50 percent every ten days, and so on. We were pursued by debt collectors demanding astronomical amounts. Debt collection was a traumatic business. It was the height of summer, and there were days when the heat was enough to melt the asphalt on the street. The heavies sent by the loan sharks couldn't care less. They ripped out all the air-conditioning units in the house and piled them up in the garage along with a bunch of other household appliances, all in full view of the neighbors, of course. Our large-sized American refrigerator was left lying on its side, its doors hanging open to reveal nothing but empty white racks. The wooden parquet floors were so damaged that they didn't lie flat anymore, creating a kind of bizarre optical illusion that the ground was moving.

Every day without fail, the debt collectors would fling open our doors or windows and yell in at us. I knew there was no point in arguing, but one day I cracked under the pressure. After one thug had just hurled a string of abuse at my mother, I brought my fist crashing down on the kitchen table.

"Who the hell do you think you're threatening? If you keep on talking to my parents like that, you stupid assholes, then that's it."

"Fucking kid!" he spat back.

So this was what it was like to have no money. I wanted to cry with frustration.

The nightmare continued right into the winter. The only source of heat left in the house was the traditional *kotatsu* heated table in my bedroom. The freezing wind blew in through the windows that the debt collectors kept on opening, and chilled us to the bone. Na-chan was terrified of one guy who used to come round snarling like a mad dog.

"Shoko, I'm scared," she'd whisper, clinging to me.

"He'll be gone soon. Let's hide under here for now."

We curled up like two cats under the warm kotatsu and, hands over our ears to keep out the shouts of the debt collector, prayed as hard as we could for him to leave. Na-chan was trembling, and I was reminded of the times when I was in elementary school and Dad used to go on his drunken rampages through the house. Na-chan would be just as terrified then. She'd come to my room and crawl into my futon with me, shaking and crying just like this. But in those days, I could tell her with confidence that it would be all right in the morning. Now I had no idea if it would ever be all right again. There was nothing I could do to help my family pay off our debts, and I was left feeling angry and helpless.

During one of his rare appearances at home, Dad came to talk to me.

"Shoko, it's all my fault. I got us into debt and now you're all paying for it. I know it's tough, but please don't give up."

"I know, Dad. It's OK."

I knew how hard this was on him. When his businesses had been going well, our family home had been bustling with people, but now only a few close associates would come visit. As our furniture and household appliances slowly disappeared, so did any signs that the house was lived in. It was as if we were living on the set of some TV soap opera where everything looked rich and opulent from the outside, but it was all an illusion for the cameras.

Women weren't supposed to be versed in the ways of the yakuza, but I understood Dad had resigned for the sake of honor. As soon as he had been burdened with these debts, he had voluntarily stepped down from his role as gang leader. He could no longer show off or flash his money around in the way that yakuza do. It was as if he was sullying the name of yakuza. Yakuza are supposed to be strong, after all. But I couldn't help wondering why he couldn't have used his influence as a yakuza to get out of paying his debts? I guess to a man like my father, that would have been shameful. I understood his way of thinking, but it was sad to see how the once-impressive tattoo on his back now looked so tiny and insignificant.

I learned all this shortly before turning seventeen.

While all this was going on at home, a bunch of us yankis went one day to hang out with a guy we knew who had just become a yakuza. As the rookie, he had been left in charge of the office, so we all turned up there with our bags of thinner. We were all nicely buzzed when one of his superiors, a guy called Nakauchi, came back unexpectedly. We managed to hide all the thinner, but we could do nothing about the smell. The place reeked. As he walked in, an incredible feeling of tension ran through the room. Nakauchi dropped onto the couch.

"When are you losers going to grow up? If you're going to get high, at least do it with the good stuff."

And with that, he produced from his leather wrist bag a four-inch-square plastic bag of speed and a syringe, and tossed them casually onto the table. It was nothing like the usual half-inch size packets that I'd seen before. This was a massive amount of drugs.

"Hey, you, go get me some water," he ordered our rookie friend, who rushed off to the kitchen to fill a glass. Nakauchi then took scissors and cut the corner off a magazine to use as a scoop for the powder. Everyone immediately lined up to get a shot, looking as if they had been doing it all their lives. I didn't know what to do, but it looked like we were all expected to take some. I couldn't be the only good girl and say

I didn't do speed, but I couldn't exactly get up and leave either.

"You're doing some too, right?" said my girlfriend Mizue, as if it was the most normal thing in the world. She had just taken her turn. When I didn't know how to answer, she smirked. "Don't tell me you never shot up before?"

"Yeah, I've done it!" I said angrily. I put on a face like I'd seen it all before, and just so my yanki friends wouldn't think I was chicken, I decided to shoot up. I wanted to look cool.

I copied the others by gripping my upper arm until a vein stood out and then I presented it to Nakauchi.

"That's a good vein," he said with a smile, then stuck the needle into my arm. When about a third of the needle had disappeared into my flesh, the syringe began to fill up with blood.

"OK, that's enough."

As I released the pressure on my upper arm, Nakauchi slowly pushed the plunger of the syringe in as far as it would go, then quickly pulled the needle out. He handed me a tissue.

"Thank you," I said, dabbing at the needle mark with the tissue. Suddenly I felt a cold rush through my whole body. It was as if my hair was standing on end.

"D'you feel that?" asked Nakauchi, as he filled the syringe with water from the glass and emptied it into an ashtray.

"Not really," I replied. I wasn't sure how I was supposed to be feeling.

"You're kidding. That's weird. It looked to me like that should have done it. You must be pretty tough. I'll give you another bump, OK?"

Nakauchi nodded to the rookie to go change the water in the glass and empty the ashtray.

"Think this'll be enough?" he asked me, pouring some of the powder onto a notebook.

I nodded, hoping I didn't look as clueless as I felt. Nakauchi put on a serious expression.

"This one's gonna be strong."

This time it hit me like lightning, rushing from the tips of my toes to the top of my head.

"Feel it now, right?"

"Yeah. It's totally different."

Mizue came over and peered at my face.

"Shoko, are you sure you're OK doing that much?"

"Yeah. No problem."

Already high on speed, we all spent the rest of the night smoking pot, laughing, and joking. However, about the time the sun came up, I began to feel short of breath, and my body, which had felt as if it was floating on air, started to feel extraordinarily heavy. The feeling of ecstasy was replaced by one of sheer agony. Now I finally began to understand why those kids back in ninth grade had been prepared to do anything to get their hands on speed. I thought about this as my body started to crash, and I watched my friends deal with their own crash by topping up with more speed. Nakauchi noticed something was wrong and came over.

"Go on, have another fix. There's plenty more where that came from."

"I'm fine. I think I'll go home now."

"Don't you think you'd better lie down for a while first?"

"Thanks for everything, but I think I'd better go."

"Fine. Come again anytime. Hey, you! Shoko's leaving. Get her a taxi."

"Yes, will do!" replied the rookie in an irritatingly cheerful tone.

"Use this to get home," said Nakauchi, slipping a ¥10,000 bill into my jacket pocket. "And give me a call when you get there."

"Sure," I answered weakly.

It wasn't long before I heard the taxi arrive. The rest of my friends said they'd hang out a while longer. It didn't matter—I just wanted to get out of that place as quickly as possible. I hastily made my excuses, pushed open the heavy iron office door, and scrambled into the waiting taxi. I was afraid the driver would notice something, so I did my best to seem completely calm. It took forever to get home.

The front door had been left open again, and I could hear the shouts of the debt collectors. It was like being back in hell. And it wasn't even a hallucination. It was harsh reality. I ran to the nearest public telephone as if something was after me.

"Hi, it's Shoko. I got home OK."

"Good. Oh, Shoko, just a minute. Nakauchi-san says he wants to speak to you."

"Shoko? Yeah, good to hear from you. Hey, you sound out of breath. Are you feeling OK?"

"Yeah, I'm fine. I couldn't call from the house, so I had to run to a public phone."

"Ha! I can't believe you managed to run in that state!" Nakauchi laughed.

"Thank you for last night."

"No problem, no problem. Drop by again soon, OK? If you don't want to come by yourself, tag along with Mizue, all right?"

"Thanks. Well, good-bye."

I hung up and set off back home. The slight uphill slope felt like a mountain climb to me.

When I got back, I found my mother's favorite white ceramic vase upturned on the floor, stand and all. It didn't make any difference whether I shot up or not—my life was still hell.

Drop-dead tired, I began to put the shoes back on their rack, even though I knew they'd just end up flung on the floor again. Then I turned the flower stand upright and began to gather up the pieces of broken vase. I let out a deep sigh. I had tried to escape one kind of living hell and ended up setting foot in a different one—the world of hard drugs. After that, on the few occasions he came home, I couldn't even look Dad in the eye anymore.

That winter, when the weather was at its coldest, the debt collectors' visits started to become even more frequent and their actions far more drastic than before. I made up my mind to go with Mizue to visit Nakauchi at his home. He'd no sooner opened the door and invited us in than Mizue set off through the apartment as if she'd been there a million times. She went straight over to a rattan sofa by the window and sat down.

"Shoko, you want some speed?" she asked.

"Are you sure it's OK?" I said, hesitantly.

"What are you talking about? That's what we came for, isn't it?"

Nakauchi laughed at Mizue and me whispering to each other.

"Shoko, you don't have to be polite. Mizue's a regular round here."

As if to prove the point, Mizue got up, made her way to the kitchen and came back with a glass of water. She got her fix, and then I followed.

From that day on, the three of us got together regularly to do speed. I'd never actually heard that Nakauchi and Mizue were a couple, but it seemed there was something going on between them, so I never hung around too long after getting my fix.

There was a day when we'd all shot up as usual, but then Nakauchi told us he had an errand to run. Mizue went to put her shoes on too.

"Oh, Shoko, so sorry—I've got to step out too. Do you mind waiting here for me? Nakauchi-san will probably be right back."

"Are you going to be long?"

"Um, not really. Why don't you play a TV game while you're waiting?"

"OK. Later!"

There was something weird about Mizue's manner that made me feel slightly anxious. Nakauchi came back about thirty minutes later. I was playing Nintendo in the back room when I heard him call out from the kitchen, "Hey, Shoko, want another fix?"

He put the needle into my left arm as I gripped with my right. The blood that backtracked into the syringe was thicker and darker than earlier in the day.

Thank you Mario! The Nintendo sang out its familiar tune.

I'd saved Princess Peach so many times she must have been absolutely ecstatic. I was sick of playing, but I had to do something to take my mind off the fact that I was alone in the apartment with Nakauchi, waiting for Mizue, who seemed to be taking forever.

"Why don't you stop playing and get something to eat," Nakauchi suggested, noticing I'd become restless.

"Thanks, I'm not hungry. I think I'd better—"

"There's no hurry. Why don't you eat something before you go?"

"Mizue's so late... You know, I think I'd better get home."

"No point in waiting for her anyway."

"What?"

"Mizue's not coming back. Come on, let's fuck."

"Hey! Get your hands off me!" I tried to get to my feet, but he held me down with incredible force.

"Stop it!"

"Don't struggle."

He ripped open my blouse and pulled up my bra.

"Don't!"

"Mizue didn't mind."

"I'm not Mizue! Get off me!"

"Do as you're told, bitch."

He hit me across the face, his heavy ring catching my left cheek. I tasted the metallic flavor of blood in my mouth. He was going to rape me and there was nothing I could do about it.

Just as I started to feel my strength ebb away, someone banged on the door.

"Nakauchi-san, let me in! Shoko?"

"Mizue!" I screamed. I pushed Nakauchi off and ran to the door.

"Shit. What the hell is she doing back?"

The moment Nakauchi opened the door, I shot out into the night without even bothering to put my shoes on. I walked home barefoot on the cold asphalt, my arms crossed to hide the huge tear in my clothing.

The next day, Mizue called.

"Shoko? I'm sorry about yesterday."

"Oh?"

"I'm really, truly sorry. I told him not to do it. I honestly told him, but..." She began to sob.

"I don't want to hear it. Bye."

What kind of a friend was she? After that, I stopped seeing Mizue and her friends, and I started to hang out with another crowd. We did speed every day.

Different debt collectors would invade our home daily, but it turned out that one of the most frequent visitors was an old acquaintance of my dad's. His name was Maejima, and he was an ex-yakuza. Maejima had made quite a bit of money as a loan shark, and had even done some official business with Dad in the past. Ironically, one of the toughs he brought along with him was a drug buddy of mine, Kimura.

One day, as they were leaving, Kimura whispered to me under his breath, "See ya," and gave me a guilty smile. He was spotted by Maejima.

"Kimura, do you know this kid?"

"Yes."

"What's your name?"

"Shoko."

"You're Shoko?" Maejima laughed in surprise.

"Yes."

"Hmm. You shouldn't play around like you do. You're really hurting your parents."

Maejima was smartly dressed in an expensive suit, and his stare was intimidating. I nodded politely in response and went to my room. Right away, I got a call from Kimura.

"Shoko, can you come out?"

"Are you alone?"

"No. I'm with Maejima-san."

"Then no way."

"Oh, come on. Maejima-san told me to invite you to dinner."

"Please, Kimura-kun, find a way to refuse for me, OK?"

"Come on, Shoko. I'll be there too. You'll be fine."

"If it was just you, it'd be OK. I'm sorry."

It wasn't just an excuse. I was afraid of meeting Maejima. After that, Kimura kept on calling to ask me out, but I somehow managed to keep putting him off. In the end, Maejima called me himself.

"Shoko, you do drugs, right? Be in front of your house at seven, OK?"

I couldn't refuse. I had in fact just come back from shooting up. I was terrified Maejima was planning to rat on me to my parents.

I hung up and hurried to fix my makeup. By seven o'clock, I was waiting in front of the gate, just as he had told me to. Maejima's Mercedes Benz appeared right on time. I got into the passenger side, and he drove off without a word. I plucked up courage to ask where we were going.

"I know this new hotel that has a karaoke machine in the room. What do you think?" he asked with a leer, one hand on my knee.

"What the fuck . . . ? Stop the car!"

"Do you know how much money your father owes?" Maejima asked, calmly continuing to drive.

"I'm sure it's a lot."

"A lot doesn't even begin to cover it! He owes me a fucking packet to start with."

"That much?"

"Yeah. Megabucks. Now, Shoko, sweetheart, you wouldn't want to see your father pushed over the edge by all those debts, would you?" His voice turned smarmy.

"No."

"It's hard on you too, I bet."

"I guess."

"I could ease the pressure some."

"Seriously?"

"Yes, but I'm not forcing you to do anything you don't want to. So... how about it? Do you still want me to let you out of the car?"

I shook my head.

"I heard you're into speed. I've got some right here."

I closed my eyes and took a deep breath. It had been a long time since I'd smelled expensive leather seats. Soon we arrived at what was clearly a "love hotel." This one was done up as a tasteless neon castle. Maejima drove into the parking lot through a black vinyl curtain, designed to keep guests anonymous. I thought I'd made up my mind to go ahead with it, but at the last minute I couldn't get out of the car. Maejima reached across me and opened the passenger door.

"Don't be such a baby. Get out."

I didn't move.

"Don't you trust me at all, Shoko?"

"Sure...but..."

As soon as we entered the hotel room, Maejima took off his tie and told me to bring him some water. I filled a glass in the bathroom and brought it to him. Then I rolled up my left sleeve and popped a vein. Maejima filled the syringe with speed, and with a practiced hand, injected it into my arm. He gave himself a fix too, then stood up.

"I'm taking a bath," he announced.

He stood up, carefully rolled down his sleeve, and started to take off his shirt. I quickly washed the syringe in the basin, then hung Maejima's suit up for him. I ran him a bath then hurried to turn on the TV.

"Come here." Maejima was calling from the bathroom.

"What?"

"Get in with me."

This was the first time I'd ever taken a bath with a man, and I was so embarrassed that my cheeks were on fire. I held a towel in front of me as I poured water over my body, then climbed into the tub, trying to keep my back to him.

"Have you ever had sex on speed?"

"No..."

"Oh baby, you haven't lived. Get your sweet ass over here and let me show you."

"Um, what we were talking about before...about my father..."

"That's all taken care of. Forget about it. You want to be my girl, right?"

"Uh...yes."

"OK. That's good. Now, you understand that you can never tell anyone about this?"

When I agreed, he snorted with laughter, groped at my breast and stuck his tongue so far into my mouth that I could hardly breathe.

"Sit here."

We got out of the bath, and Maejima made me sit on the low wooden stool next to the tub, while he soaped my body from head to toe. There was a tattoo on his back of a creepy-looking kabuki character entwined with a dragon. Through the mist of the shower, the dragon looked as if it was spewing out clouds of steam. I felt as if I was in the middle of a bad dream. I shut my eyes tightly as Maejima's face moved toward mine.

After the bath, Maejima had another fix. He told me to do the same, and when I held out my left arm, he coaxed out the same vein as before and stuck the needle in. The moment he pulled it out, everything went black for a second, and I was terrified that I'd gone blind. After that, all I could do was lie on the bed, unable to move. Maejima tried everything to get me turned on, but my body refused to react, and in the end he gave up. The last thing I remember was him looking totally bummed, and then it was morning.

"Considering how wild you're supposed to be, you're not exactly good in bed, are you?" he said with a smirk. "Never mind, you're about to learn from the master. Once you've done it with me on speed, baby, you'll never be able to do it any other way." But I knew that was a lie. I wasn't in love with this guy, so how could sex ever be any good with him?

From then on, we went to a love hotel almost every night, shot up, and then had sex. At first, I would lie there passively, but one night my body actually responded. I felt myself getting wet, and as he entered me, all the blood in my veins seemed to rush to one spot, and I felt an intense buildup of heat. I found myself clinging to Maejima's body and crying out in pleasure.

Before I met Maejima, sex had been a cold, passionless business. Even though guys had seemed to have a genuine interest in me, once sex was over, that was the end of it. I had never been treated well by anyone—I'd only done it a few times with some random guys who weren't even boyfriends. Now I had found out what it was like to have an orgasm.

From then on, just seeing the backtrack of blood in the syringe when Maejima shot up was enough to get me turned on.

"Do me... Come on, I want it now," I would beg, and we'd do it all night.

Yet no matter how much speed I took, I refused to let anyone call me a speed freak. In my gang there had been several kids who had become addicted, and we'd stopped trusting them. Only other addicts would spend any time with them. When they talked, you'd think *Oh, they're just wasted*, and ignore everything they said. And bad rumors spread like wildfire. Even if you never touched the stuff, if someone started a rumor then that was it for you. Nobody wanted a speed freak as a friend.

One of my friends had got so messed up from his speed habit that he'd become delusional. He'd convinced himself that his girlfriend was cheating on him, and set her house on fire. And that his pores were infested with maggots—he slashed his own skin with a box cutter. He spent hours on end squeezing his speed bumps—those zits that people on speed get—until his skin became sore and festering. He was convinced someone was watching him, so he covered all the windows in his home with packing tape. He kept all his appliances unplugged, believing this would stop "them" from tapping his home. He decided he could hear his neighbors' voices bad-mouthing him, so he'd rush out of his front door barefooted and brandishing a knife, but of course, there'd be nobody there. He'd slink down the street, constantly peering over his shoulder, convinced a detective was following him. Whenever he drove anywhere, he'd look obsessively in his rearview mirror at the car behind him. Ironically, because he believed he was being chased by the yakuza, he would even take refuge at the police station.

Information would travel at high speed through the network of users: who had been busted, who had a warrant out on them, who was under investigation and had to be avoided, whose home had been raided. You can get really pure stuff at this place. At that place, it's cut with too much other shit. Where to score, who's recently started using, who's kicked the habit...

I didn't want to hear it, I didn't want to see it, I didn't want to know about it. I didn't want them to know about me. I didn't want to be one of them.

But getting high with Maejima helped me to block out the misery that was my home life. Whenever I was stuck at home, my mother sobbing as the debt collectors banged on the door, and Na-chan clinging to me in terror, I would long to see that backtrack of blood in the syringe and know that I was about to escape reality.

The needle dug into my vein, but just as Maejima was about to push the plunger in, it sprang back out.

"Shit. Your vein keeps moving. I can't get it in."

He pulled out the needle and tapped my arm furiously until it bruised. Finally, a vein reappeared. When he stuck the needle in again, dark blood flowed back up like dirty river scum, and my body started drifting out to sea.

"How's that? You loaded?"

"Mm."

"It's taking a lot to get you there these days. You need as much as me."

I sighed and lit Maejima's cigarette for him.

"Get those clothes off and get over here," ordered Maejima, flinging back the bedcovers.

I held him as tightly as I could and murmured, "I want you so much."

"Yeah, I'm kinda getting to like you too, Shoko."

Whispering my name, he slipped a wet tongue in my ear. For some reason an image came to my mind of playing in our pool as a kid and the sound of the water splashing. I remembered the games I would play with Maki. She'd dare me to try and hold my breath and swim a whole lap underwater. I used to love swimming underwater and the feeling of being in another world.

Hey, you losers, if you lay a finger on my little sister, I'll get you!

She was always saving me from bullies.

Who needs friends when you have your big sister with you?

The image of Maki's face began to fade...

"Does that feel good, baby?"

"Mm. Don't stop."

Another water memory came back to me. This time it was feeding the koi in our family's pond. They would always react to the sound of my footsteps and come scrambling toward me.

Calm down. There's plenty of food for all of you.

The fish would frantically leap on top of each other to get at the little pellets of feed, sending water spraying into the air. I loved this daily routine of taking care of my fish.

My memories began to merge with sordid reality. At first my mind had been pleasantly drifting as I lay on the circular love hotel bed, but suddenly I was struggling as I sank down to a murkier, more frightening place.

CHAPTER FOUR

Lovers

I had taken a job at a small neighborhood bar working four hours, twice a week. It wasn't long before I started dating one of my customers. Shin was eight years older than me and had just started out in his own business—but he was married. He was unlike anyone I had ever met before, and I was immediately attracted to this cool, laid-back man who seemed totally secure in his own skin. I thought about him every second of every day, but getting together was never easy, and I spent hours on end waiting for the phone to ring. As time dragged by, I would get more and more antsy. Then the excitement I felt when I picked up would turn to despair if it wasn't Shin on the other end. I was so crazy about him that sometimes it felt as if I would burst if I didn't tell him how I felt, but instead I had to act like an adult and pretend to be cool with the situation. I longed to spend the whole night with him, even just once, but I guessed that if I ever tried to push him into anything, I'd lose him completely. So I kept my mouth shut.

Since Shin had been on the scene, I'd done my best to avoid Maejima, but he kept calling up and demanding to see me. I decided that I couldn't avoid him forever, so I agreed to let him pick me up in the usual spot in front of our house. As soon as I was sitting in his car, I took a deep breath and told him the truth.

"I've met someone else."

"And?"

"I can't see you anymore."

"I don't think I quite get it. You were so into me and so desperate to go out with me that I gave in and agreed to be your boyfriend."

"So you don't mind if I break it off, then?"

"Out of the question," replied Maejima, tapping his foot in irritation as he lit his cigarette.

"Please, I'm begging you."

"OK, if you feel that strongly, go ahead—date him."

"Are you sure you're OK with it?"

"Dumb bitch! Can't you see that works out even better for me?"

"What are you talking about?"

"Don't you get it?"

"You mean if I've got another boyfriend, my folks'll be less likely to find out about you?"

"Oh, finally, the light comes on!"

"Right, take me home now!"

"Oh baby, take it easy. I'll take you straight home, don't worry. And you don't mind if I mention to Daddy that his little girl is a total speed freak, do you?"

"Then you'd be in just as much shit as me."

"Oh no, I don't think so. Not when I tell him how I caught you shooting up with all those other losers and brought you safely back home. I imagine they'll be falling over themselves to thank me, don't you?"

"Look, just leave my father out of this. He trusts you completely."

"Of course he does. With all those debts to worry about and working like a dog to pay them off, I'm sure it'd kill him to find out I was fucking his darling Shoko."

"What if I told him everything?"

"Go ahead. There's nowhere else left for him a squeeze a penny from. If it wasn't for me, he'd be finished. I thought you understood that better than anyone, Shoko."

"Yeah, I guess…"

"So we're agreed then—we're not breaking up."

"But I can't—"

"What are you talking about? Who's the one who gets high and begs 'do me, do me' like she's going to burst into tears if I don't?"

"Shut up!"

"Hey kid, don't you fucking sass me, OK?"

There was nothing more to say.

In my circle of friends, there were no other girls involved with married men. They were all free to walk openly hand in hand on the street with their boyfriends. They'd knit them sweaters or scarves for birthday presents, and carry photos in their wallets of them kissing. Their boyfriends would pick them up after school in their cool, spray-painted hot rods. They'd more or less live together under their parents' roofs. I'd never been able to walk in public with either Maejima or Shin. I couldn't let anyone see them, and I couldn't talk about them to anyone. My friends' lives seemed as far removed as the moon I'd seen from the detention center window. I didn't belong anywhere.

At night, when Shin used to drop me off at home, I'd always wish we could spend a little longer together, and it was hard for me to open the door and go into the house. This was the first time I'd ever felt this way. Even if Shin wasn't serious about me, I didn't care—I just wanted to be with him.

On my eighteenth birthday, Shin got me the most unbelievable present. We were out driving, when he stopped the car in front of a brand-new apartment building and told me to get out. I followed him into the elevator and we got off at the fifth floor. He walked up to the corner apartment and produced two keys. He handed one to me.

"Go on, open it."

I tried the key in the lock. There was a click, and the door swung open.

"I can't believe it. Is this for me?"

"Yes. And you don't have to worry about the rent or the bills. I'll take care of it all. Why don't you quit that job?"

"But I—"

"It's the only way we'll have time to meet."

"So if I quit, you'll be able to come and see me in the evenings?"

"Right. I'll be able to call in on the way home from work, even if it's only for a few minutes."

"Are you serious? I can live here?"

"Think of it as a present for both of us. I know it's been hard on you, but maybe we can start over... Happy birthday." He took me in his arms and held me tight.

"It hasn't been that bad. I'm just happy to see you at all."

The sex I had with Shin was warm and loving. Making love with him was the only time I felt as if I had anything in common with my friends and the normal, romantic relationships they had with their boyfriends. Any pleasure I got from the sex I had with Maejima was tied up with things like drugs, money, and betrayal of my parents. When I was having sex on speed, all I needed or wanted or could focus on was the physical pleasure I got with the buzz from the drugs. More to the point, I couldn't face sex with Maejima without being on it. Shin was the only person I knew who could actually love someone as messed up as me. But he would always go home as soon as we'd made love. I knew that deep down he didn't really need me, and tears would come to my eyes every time I watched him leave.

The next day, I quickly gathered together all my possessions and started my life as a "kept woman." I felt as though I had escaped from Maejima. Unfortunately, Shin soon got even busier than before, and there were whole weeks when he wouldn't set foot in the apartment or even be able to call. It was pretty ironic that he'd bought it just so we could spend more time together. I was dying to do some speed, but instead I would grit my teeth and try to wait it out alone. The apartment had that peculiar smell of fresh paint that new buildings have, and without much furniture, the place felt cold and empty.

One day, I had just stepped out of the building when I heard a familiar voice call out, "Hey, Shoko!" I immediately froze in my tracks. Apparently, it had been a simple task for Maejima to hunt me down. His black Mercedes pulled up alongside me.

"Get in."

I shook my head.

"Just fucking do it, OK?"

This time I obeyed.

"What's up with you? Don't you need a fix?"

"Don't come around here, OK?"

"What the fuck are you talking about? You're free to see whoever you want. And I know you want to see me, don't you, baby?"

Just like that first night, I didn't speak a word during the drive to the love hotel. But once we were inside the room, I tried to talk to him.

"Look, I really don't want to see you anymore."

"Don't give me that shit!" Maejima grabbed an ashtray off the table and threw it at me. It hit me in the forehead and gouged out a piece of flesh. When he saw me trying to wipe away the blood that was trickling down into my eye, he put out his hand to help me.

"Get the fuck away from me!" I yelled, knocking his hand away.

"Shoko, baby, that look on your face—you sure take after your father.

OK, listen to me. I won't come to your apartment again, all right?"

"I hate you!"

"If this is how you want it, your family can pay me back the money you owe me right now," he said, suddenly more threatening. "If you fuck me around, it's you that's gonna suffer."

I didn't reply.

"I don't ever want to see my girl with a look like that on her face again. Do you understand me?"

"Yes..."

"I'm glad we understand each other." He began to get the syringe ready, an infuriatingly smug expression on his face. "Arm!" he ordered.

"I don't want any."

"Are you still fucking with me?"

He picked up the glass of water and threw the whole thing at me, then kicked me in the stomach. I fell to the floor and my right hand landed on a piece of broken glass. It sliced open my middle finger. There were track marks of blood on the floor where I had put out my hand to steady myself. I stayed down near the ground, holding my stomach. But Maejima wasn't finished yet.

"Don't ever piss me off again!" He picked up the thermos of hot water next to the teapot and hurled it to the floor. The scalding water splashed onto my hand, burning the skin between my ring finger and little finger. I got unsteadily to my feet and took two towels from the bathroom. I used one to bind the cut on my hand and wiped away the blood from my forehead with the other. Then, ignoring the pain, I began to clear up the room, while Maejima sat calmly on the sofa, shooting up. Just seeing the needle made my toes curl and my palms start to sweat. I knew I had to resist, but I wanted some so badly...

"Shit, I can't get it in. Give me your left arm...tighter!" Maejima waited for the backtrack, then unloaded the syringe into my arm.

"How's that feel?" Maejima's voice was just a faint echo. "I bet you're horny—"

I didn't wait for him to finish speaking. I flung myself on him.

"What is it you want from me, baby?"

"Fuck me."

"I'm sorry, I didn't quite catch that. A bit louder."

"Fuck me. Please!"

"You should have just said that in the first place. You know you're just going to beg me for it the minute you shoot up."

"Yeah."

"Going on about breaking up and other crap..."

Just being held so tightly was enough to make me moan.

"You really need me, don't you Shoko?"

But I couldn't stand to hear these words from the man who was betraying my father.

The misfit who had been bullied at school, the innocent child who was almost raped by Mizuguchi, the dutiful daughter who would help Mom clean up with after one of Dad's rampages, the little kid who always had to watch out she didn't get Dad mad, none of these were the real me. I used to think about the events of my childhood as if they'd happened to someone else. It was much easier that way. But I had ended up reinventing myself too many times, and now it was impossible to tell who the real Shoko was. I was able to disconnect my heart and mind from my body and lose myself in the thrill I could get from Maejima and speed. But still, whenever each drug-fueled date with Maejima was about to come to an end and the thrill wore off, I was left feeling hollow of any emotion, save guilt toward Shin.

"I can't do this."

Maejima looked totally unconcerned. "It's just a matter of time before you and this other guy split up. There's no way he could satisfy a slut like you," he laughed.

A matter of time... There was nothing I needed more than to spend time with Shin right now.

Soon after that, Shin turned up at the apartment for the first time in ages, and noticed right away there was something strange about me.

"Shoko! Show me your arm!" he ordered. He caught hold of my hand and pushed up my sleeve. There were the telltale needle tracks in my scrawny arm.

"You've been shooting up. What the hell were you thinking?" This was the first time I'd ever seen Shin lose his cool. "I can't believe you'd do drugs."

"I want to stop. But I just can't quit. Help me. Please." I buried my face in my hands. Shin put his arms around me and hugged me tightly.

"Look, Shoko, I know you're seeing someone else. What right have I got to tell you not to see other people? But shooting up? Please promise me you'll quit right now."

"I'm sorry."

"I love you, Shoko. I really love you." That was what I needed to hear. "I worry about you when I'm not around, but I can't be with you all the time. I really wish I could, but I can't. Please understand."

I nodded reluctantly. I understood. But he was never there when I needed him. Without so much as a phone call for two weeks at time, our relationship had too much empty space. I seemed to wait forever to see him, and then our time together would be over in an instant. I was always afraid to let go of his hand because I never knew when I'd get to hold it again.

There were some happy times. I loved hearing him say my name and having him hold me in his arms. The city always seemed dull and gray when I walked alone, but when I was with Shin, my senses were heightened. In spring, I would notice the cherry blossom petals floating everywhere on the soft breeze. In summer I'd hear the tinkling of wind chimes and be reminded of the times I used to sit with Mom or Dad on the porch enjoying the cool evening breeze. In fall, we'd be enveloped by the heavy scent of the golden osmanthus blossoms. In winter, if Shin called, I'd happily wait out in the street for him, exhaling clouds of white breath, my ears tingling with the cold. I remember one time he was particularly late, but I stayed outside until he finally arrived.

"Sorry! I just couldn't get away. You could have waited inside. You're going to freeze to death out here." Shin wrapped his arms around my frozen body.

"Just a little longer... Just stay like that..."

"Shoko, I know this is all hard for you, but I honestly do love you. Tell me you won't ever break up with me. You know I can't leave my wife, but I can't stop wanting to be with you either. I'm so selfish..."

"No you're not. I'm the one who's being selfish." After all, I was constantly cheating on Shin too.

"Shoko." He took my face in both hands and kissed me tenderly.

The drug honeymoon was over—my fucked-up body was well and truly hooked on speed. And to make matters worse, now Maejima began to flip out. If there was ever a time he couldn't get in touch with me, he would go ballistic, and once he found me, we'd be holed up in a love hotel for two or three days at a time. I wasn't even allowed to set foot out of the room. He used to throw me onto the bed and go into a long rant about how I'd been avoiding him. When I tried to answer back, he'd call me a liar and kick the hell out of me.

One time, he'd been beating up on me as usual, when suddenly he stopped.

"Don't even fucking think about touching that phone until I get back!" he barked out. He slammed the door behind him, leaving me lying on the bed, moaning in pain.

He returned a couple of hours later with a paper shopping bag in one hand. We went through our usual routine of shooting up together, but then he took the bathrobe belt that he'd been using to pop a vein, and bound my hands together.

"What are you doing? Let me go!"

"Wanna try this?" he asked with a leer, producing a vibrator and a bottle of lubricant from the paper bag.

"No way!"

"Come on baby, you know you want to."

"Get off me, you pervert!" I yelled, and got a punch in the face. There was a sickening crunch, and warm blood began to seep from my ear.

"Relax your legs."

"Stop, please..."

"Shit, I can't get it in." Maejima gave up with the vibrator and instead began to spread lubricant over my body, grossing me out as he rubbed and slobbered all over me. After subjecting me to this for about an hour, he finally forced the vibrator inside me.

"That hurts!"

"Just hang in there, it'll start feeling good."

I gave up struggling.

"Feel any better?"

"I'd rather have you."

"Yeah? I'm better than this?"

"Yes...do me." Even after all this, I still had to have him. "Come on, please!"

"No, baby, I wanna watch you do yourself with this."

"I can't."

"It's nothing to be embarrassed about. Come on, sweetheart, do it for me." He untied my hands and passed me the vibrator.

"No."

"Oh, just give it me. I'll make you come." He snatched it back from me, forced me to turn over, and shoved it back inside me.

I let out a small groan.

This got Maejima all excited. "Louder, come on, I want to hear you moan."

I forced myself to play along. "Mmm, yes!"

"So, does that feel good now?"

"Yeah."

"Come on, Shoko. Do it for me, baby." He handed me the vibrator again.

"Mmm."

"No, look, it's better like this." Maejima put his hand over mine and began to jiggle the vibrator wildly around inside me. "Open your legs wider. I can't see."

"Oh...God!"

"Come on, I want you to be really nasty. Come on, baby, stick it all the way in."

"Please. Do me now." I pulled Maejima on top of me and we started fucking like crazy. Sitting in the taxi on the way back to my apartment, I fingered the cuts and bruises on my face. Fresh blood began to ooze from the cut on my mouth. How low could I sink? A shiver ran down my spine as I thought about what I was doing.

One time, Maejima got a big payoff or something, and was in an unusually cheerful mood. He used the phone in the love hotel to call up some woman he knew who was a speed user and went by the name of Saori. When she turned up, he told her to "perform" with me while he watched. When I looked puzzled, he whispered in my ear, "She's a lesbian, so you don't need to do anything if you don't want to. Just let her do her thing."

I nodded weakly and got on the bed. Saori took off my bathrobe and began to lick my ear. Her tongue in my mouth and her soft hands on my skin felt totally different from a man's. Then, while she gently ran her tongue over my body, she slipped a finger inside me and began thrusting it in and out.

"Shoko, turn your face this way and make some noise!" Maejima was like some customer at a sleazy sex show as he smoked his cigarette and catcalled. Saori reacted to his words and began to thrust her finger furiously and lick me harder than ever.

"Ah, no, I'm gonna...please, come here!" I stretched out a hand to Maejima.

"OK, you can get out of here." Maejima stood up and dragged Saori off the bed. He took a pile of ¥10,000 bills from his wallet and casually tossed them at her.

"So you want me that much?" he asked, stroking my face as he climbed on top of me.

"I want you now...hurry!" I answered, wrapping my arms around his body.

"Oh Shoko, that's good, that feels so good," he murmured. As he began to thrust inside me, he turned to Saori and made a shooing gesture with his hand. She scrambled to gather up the bills from the floor, got dressed, and left the room.

That was the day Maejima started to pressure me to break up with Shin.

"Isn't it about time you got rid of this guy?"

When I simply shook my head, he asked, "Are you trying to piss me off?"

"No, Maejima-san, I don't want to upset you..."

"Look, I take care of all your needs. I buy you whatever you want, don't I, sweetheart?"

"I just can't be with you anymore."

"I treat you like a fucking queen."

"You don't give a shit about me."

"What do you mean, I don't give a shit?"

"If you cared that much, you'd let me go."

"No can do. You think we can break up, and that'll be the end of it. Obviously, a brat like you has no idea how much money I've invested in this relationship. I'm not just playing around here. You can't let me do all this for you and then turn around and tell me you want to end it."

There was an awkward silence. Maejima reached over and stroked my cheek. "You're so cute, I just can't help it."

"Get your hands off me!"

"Don't give me that crap again. Who the fuck do you think you're talking to?" Without warning, he slapped me hard across the face.

"I want to break up."

"Fucking stubborn brat!" The force of Maejima's kick sent me flying into the table. My eye made contact with the corner, and what felt like tears began to trickle from it. I put my hand to my face and realized it was blood.

"We're so through!" I said in disgust.

"Wrong. I'm not the one you're through with!" This time Maejima grabbed me by the hair and slammed my head on the floor. It felt as though someone was pressing a hot iron rod into my skull.

"Please don't...I'm sorry," I stammered.

"You want me to forgive you? You can get down on your knees and beg for my forgiveness!"

I'd hurt Maejima's pride, and he couldn't control his rage. He pinned my head to the floor with his foot. My head was already killing me from his last attack, and now the extra pressure on my already throbbing skull made me explode in fury.

"You want *me* to beg *your* forgiveness? Go ahead—hit me all you like. There's no way in hell I'm ever going to apologize to you."

"Fine. Have it your way. I've had it with all your bullshit anyway—being around you is starting to mess with my head. Do what the fuck you like."

But Maejima knew I'd be back. As time passed, my withdrawal symptoms were getting worse, and I needed more and more speed to keep them away. I was totally dependent on him. There was no escape for me.

There was another time, I think it was around the beginning of fall, when Maejima put on a hard porn video and ordered me to copy whatever the actress in it did. At first, I watched the screen in silence, but after a while the woman lying there pleasuring herself with a vibrator began to look like me. I had to look away.

"Hey, you're not watching!"

"Is...is that me?"

"What?"

"That woman. It's me."

"Shoko? What are you talking about?"

"Stop! Stop it!"

The panting noises from the TV, the hum of the refrigerator, every sound was turning into my own voice.

"Turn it off!" I threw the remote control at the TV screen and put my hands over my ears. Maejima looked at me in amazement. "What's up with you? That's not you."

"Yes it is!"

"You're crashing, baby. You'd better have another fix."

I shook my head. I was shivering all over.

"If you don't, you're really going to schitz out."

And it didn't stop with seeing myself in a porn movie. I decided the wall mirror was two-way and that someone was on the other side, ogling us as we had sex.

"Shoko, give me your arm."

I began to shake my head wildly. "No...I don't want to. I don't want to!"

"You're going to have to. You've started talking crazy."

Now I was hallucinating that some kind of bugs were crawling up and down my back, and I still couldn't get the sound of my own panting voice out of my head. In the end, I was so terrified that I held out my right arm and got my fix. The next time I turned to look at the screen all I saw was an anonymous porn actress, her legs spread for some actor. I sighed with relief, took a sip of water, and lay down on the bed.

"How're you feeling? Has it gone away?"

"Yeah..."

"You gonna eat something?" asked Maejima, picking up the menu from the table.

"I feel like ramen noodles."

"Yeah, I'll have that too. Order it, will you?"

I picked up the bedside phone and ordered two bowls of ramen.

"I can't remember the last time I saw you eat anything," Maejima remarked.

"No, I don't have much of an appetite these days."

I went to pick up the ramen that room service left outside the door and put the bowls on the table. The drugs always made my tongue sensitive to heat, so I had to wait until the soup cooled down and the noodles had turned soggy before I could eat any at all. I smoked a cigarette then joined Maejima in the bath. We fucked all night.

My phone was ringing.

"Yes?"

"Hi, Shoko. How are you doing?"

"Good. What's up, Yukie?"

"I'm doing great, but you've been acting weird lately. No one's seen you for ages and you sound kinda depressed. Have you got a cold or something?"

"No, I'm fine."

"Is there a problem? Can you talk now?"

"I told you, it's nothing."

"Well, if you're really doing OK... Hey, wanna get together with the old gang? Everyone's dying to see you. Without you around it's no fun. You always used to crack us up."

"Thanks."

If I could, I'd have gone right over to Yukie's place. But the state I was in these days, I didn't want to see anyone. I didn't feel like one of them anymore. I wished I could go back to that time when we could all have a blast together. I hated myself for not being able to get off speed.

Soon after that, Shin turned up at the apartment.

"Congratulations."

"Why?"

"Oh, come on. You've got to remember your own birthday!"

I spent every single day the same way—strung out on speed—so I had completely forgotten that today was my nineteenth birthday. Shin had bought me perfume.

"Did you choose it yourself?"

"Of course."

I took off the cap and breathed in. The scent was sweet and sensual— very grown-up.

"Thank you. Look, I'm sorry, I..."

"Sh. It's OK."

Shin knew what I'd been doing. But he thought that I had turned to another man because I was lonely, and in the process ended up addicted to speed. He was always getting mad with me about it.

"Shoko, tell me the truth. There must be a reason you're doing drugs."

I stared at the floor and said nothing.

"Why do you do it? Can't you talk to me about it?"

"Sorry," was all I could say. Then, as always, he said, "Please get off the drugs, OK?" and wrapped his arms around me. I knew it was selfish, but I secretly wished he'd be even madder at me. That he'd be passionately jealous and tell me that he wanted me to be his woman and no one else's. He always treated me so well, but I could never quite get what was going on inside his head. Yes, I was just a kid after all. I had to come to terms with the fact I'd never be on the same wavelength as this man. Still, I could understand enough to read the hidden message in this elegant bottle of scent. He was hoping that I would grow up quickly—and it hurt me horribly that I couldn't.

And then Shin started to make gentle love to me. Every touch drove me wild and I began to moan and beg him to do it harder. Suddenly he stopped and looked at me.

"Shoko! You're high right now, aren't you?"

"What?"

"I can tell when you are. Your reactions aren't the same at all."

His words made me feel dirty. The innocent version of me, the girl who had walked happily hand in hand with Shin, no longer existed.

That night I had a strange dream about my grandpa. I couldn't see his face clearly, but I was sure it was him. He was standing in the bluish mist at the top of a mountain, dressed in a white kimono. He had a sad expression on his face and was calling out, "Shoko, Shoko," gesturing to me to come to him. I woke with a start. Was Grandpa so worried about me doing drugs and sleeping with a married man that he'd appeared in my dream? Was he telling me that if I kept on this way, I might as well join him? My chest felt constricted, and I couldn't breathe. "Grandpa, I'm sorry," I whispered. But my heart, tossed around between Shin and Maejima, had been smashed into too many pieces, and I didn't know how to repair the damage.

CHAPTER FIVE

Retribution

A few days after my birthday, I got a phone call from Na-chan. "Shoko-chan, the cat died. We wrapped her in a towel and buried her under the cherry tree. We'll never see her again, but at least she'll enjoy the blossoms in spring. She'll be happy there, won't she...?"

Na-chan began to cry. Our house had been seized by the bankruptcy court, and we were being evicted. In the middle of the frenzy of moving out of the house we had loved and that held so many memories for us, our family cat had curled up in a corner of the front hall and passed away. It was as if she knew exactly what was happening. Our old dog, who had always been my friend when things got tough, had also been laid to rest under the cherry tree. Now I would never be able to touch that tree or feed the fish again. I'd never go back to the house where we had sat and laughed and eaten meals together. It felt as if our family home had come crashing down around our ears. I was the lucky one—I already had another place to live—but it still hit me hard. In fact, it was this that finally made me realize how important my family was to me. It was also the wake up call I needed to give up drugs for good.

Several days earlier, Maejima had taken me to a love hotel as usual. The evening of the second day, I told him I wanted to go home, and he freaked out.

"So you hate me that much?" he screamed, and hit me across the face. The force of the blow knocked me off the bed, and he sprang after me, kicked me in the ribs, then took hold of me by the hair and pulled me to my feet.

"Well, go on. Have you got anything else you want to say to me?" he spat. I tried to speak, but I couldn't catch my breath after the impact of the kick. "There's no way you're getting out of here." Maejima was all worked up now. He took the syringe and emptied a huge dose of speed into my arm. The moment he pulled the needle out, my face began to sweat and my body turned to jelly. My chest was on fire, and I pressed a hand to my heart to try to calm it, but it was no use. I collapsed onto the black love-hotel sheets.

"Hey, you OK?" Maejima's face was a pale blur.

"Uh-uh." I could barely get a sound out.

"Shoko!"

"C...can't breathe."

"Hey! C'mon, I didn't do anything. It's not my fault."

I could only manage a gurgling noise from the back of my throat.

"Stop kidding around... Hey, I'm sure you'll feel better in a while... Um, I've got to get going now. Later, OK?"

"Wait, Maejima-san!" My voice was no more than a whisper.

He never even looked back.

I went to get up, but my arms and legs were numb and I could barely move. But there was no way I was going to die in a place like this.

"Dad, Mom, help me!" I gasped for air and clawed hopelessly at my throat. It felt as if invisible hands were strangling me from inside. After a while, the feeling miraculously began to come back to my fingers and toes. Somehow I managed to crawl off the bed. My hand was trembling and my eyes were unfocused as I tried to apply some makeup to cover the marks around my eye where Maejima had hit me.

What a sucker I'd been. Every time he beat me up, all he had to say was "I love you," and I'd manage to turn a blind eye to the abuse. But those three little words had been the rope that bound me, and there had never been any affection in them. Right to the end, I was nothing but a toy to fill his sexual needs. I left the dark, windowless hotel room, which now seemed as empty as the lies he'd been feeding me.

For the next two days, I lay in my apartment dying to shoot up. Just staring at the tracks on my arms was enough to give me flashbacks. This was when I got the phone call from Na-chan, and it hit me that now was my chance to free myself from drugs for good.

Going cold turkey was tough. First, I suffered from constant hallucinations. I saw and heard some horrific things, and I couldn't sleep at all. Finally, after three days, the hallucinations went away, and I got my appetite back too. In fact, I couldn't stop eating. I'd down two huge bowls of rice with deep-fried pork on top and chug a two-liter bottle of water. Then I'd immediately fall asleep. I'd wake up thirsty again, drink more water, then take a steaming hot bath that would make the sweat pour off me. Then I'd eat tons of food again and go back to sleep. I spent ten days like this before I finally lost my raging appetite and felt as if my body was back to normal. This was how I escaped from the hell that was speed addiction, and after only a short time, I got the news that I'd escaped another. Less than a month after he'd left me for dead in the love hotel, Maejima died of lung congestion.

Not long after getting clean from drugs, I got a job at a hostess bar—one of those expensive places where businessmen go in the evenings to relax and chat with the young women who serve them. This was 1987 and the height of the bubble era, when Japan's economy was booming and money flowed as freely as the sake we poured for our clients. I was amazed at the way some of the businessmen spent like there was no tomorrow.

Unfortunately for Shin, his company was in some financial trouble, so he wasn't sending me money anymore. I managed to put aside a little of my salary every month and send it to my parents. Even though the rest of Japan was on a wild spending spree, things seemed to be destined to go wrong for me and my loved ones, and eventually Shin's company went bankrupt. Of course, it didn't matter to me that Shin was penniless—I loved him, and it never crossed my mind to break up with him.

I was having a hard time making ends meet too. A hostess has to spend a lot of money on her appearance, and a large percentage of my salary went for clothes, shoes, hairstyling, and makeup. There were times I'd cut back on living expenses so that I could send my parents some cash, and my budget might not stretch to food that day. But I never brought up the subject of my family with Shin, and would cheerfully act as if nothing was wrong.

My parents and Na-chan had moved to a small rented house, and my brother had found an apartment close by. Dad was still in poor health, and his only income came from some very basic manual labor on building sites. Mom got a job as a cleaner in a love hotel. She was getting on in years and wasn't used to this kind of work, and her hands got all rough and cracked. There was nothing left of the silky smooth hand that had clasped mine that day in the family court. I was almost twenty—an adult—and I felt helpless watching my parents struggle.

Every evening, I'd ignore the bitter winter wind in my face and my coat clinging to my legs from dry static as I hurried to the bar. Working was my new addiction. One night, a new client by the name of Kuramochi called me over. I gave him the usual smiling welcome, but as I sat down next to him, my heart skipped a beat. He was short, and not particularly good-looking, but there was something about him. It felt like love at first sight. He told me he was the president of a real estate company in Hirakata, just outside Osaka. He was in this area of the city on business, and was staying in a hotel close to the bar. We hit it off right away—he was the kind of guy who made you feel safe.

"Do you want to go and get a bite to eat after you finish work?"

"OK. The bar's about to close anyway."

"I'll settle the bill and wait for you out front."

"I'll be right there."

Kuramochi paid and left the bar while the song that signaled closing time, *Sotto oyasumi*, was still playing. The moment the song finished, I threw on my coat and ran out to join him.

"Sorry. You must have been cold out here."

"No problem. So, Shoko, what do you want? What do you feel like eating?"

"Well, what do you like?"

"Hmm. Let's see... You know, I don't know Sakai very well. Why don't you take me to one of your usual hangouts?"

We had dinner at one of my favorite family-style restaurants, and just as I was thinking about getting home, Kuramochi made a suggestion.

"I'm going back to my hotel now, but I really don't want to be alone. I promise I'm not going to try anything, but would you come along to keep me company?"

"What?"

"Will you come back to my room?"

"No, thanks."

"Look, I promise I'm not going to do anything."

"Honestly?"

"Honestly."

"In that case, all right." I held out my little finger.

"I feel like a kid," laughed Kuramochi, sealing the deal by linking pinkies.

"Link your pinky, and if you lie, eat a thousand pins and then you'll die," I recited. When I released his finger, he was still laughing. I didn't think he was lying to me. We'd only just met, but already I felt I could trust him. We sat and talked in his hotel room and completely lost track of time. The fact that I knew something about the real estate business through my dad put him in a good mood, and he told me about his current projects, plans for the future, and funny stories about his employees and colleagues. I really felt comfortable chatting with him, and was as relaxed as I'd ever felt.

"You know, I picked you out from the other girls at the bar right away. I really liked the look of you the minute I saw you."

"Thank you."

"Shoko, do you like sex?" he suddenly asked.

"Of course I like it," I answered truthfully.

"Well, that's putting it bluntly! Well if you really do like it, what do you think of being my girlfriend?"

"I don't know you well enough yet."

"If I told you I'd look after you, would that help?"

I didn't say anything, and Kuramochi reached out and took my hand. He looked intently into my eyes. "I'll pay for everything. I'll even buy you a house if you'll come back with me tomorrow. Leave everything to me. You know, I've played around a lot up till now, but with you I'm serious. How about it?"

It was an incredible opportunity, but I hadn't a clue how to answer. If I did what he said, and went with him there and then, my parents would probably never have to struggle to make a living again. Yet I couldn't get Shin's face out of my head.

"Please, give me time to think. Can we get together another time and talk it over some more?" I gently slipped his hand out of mine and placed it back on his knee.

He laughed uncomfortably. "I see. It's too sudden, isn't it? But next time we meet, promise you'll spend the night with me, OK? I've got to get to work now, but can I talk to you on my cell phone on the way home? You can keep me company on the long drive."

Light was creeping in through the crack between the curtains. It was already morning.

"Don't you have anyone else to talk to?" I asked with a grin, and Kuramochi laughed. Then as I was leaving, he turned to me. "I'm sorry I made you spend the whole night with me. Take this," he said, holding out ¥500,000. Never mind that this was the bubble era—it was a shocking amount of money.

"I can't take all that. We're going to meet again, aren't we? That's enough for me." I tried to hand it back.

"Don't say anything. Just take it."

"Please, don't try to make me."

"Are you still arguing?"

"I can't accept this."

"I'll stop you talking!" And to my amazement, he grabbed me and planted a big kiss on my mouth. "That shut you up." For a moment, we stood and stared at each other.

"Thank you."

"I'm going to call as soon as you get home, so be sure to pick up."

"Sure."

Just as he'd promised, the phone rang as soon as I walked in through the apartment door. It was very rare to have a cell phone in Japan at that time, but Kuramochi didn't seem to be remotely bothered about the cost, and he talked to me all the way to his office on the other side of Osaka. We made plans to meet in a week and finally hung up.

The next day was Sunday. I went to visit my parents and handed Mom the ¥500,000.

"Where did you get this much money?" she asked me suspiciously.

"I didn't do anything bad to get it. I want you to have it."

"Well, if you're sure... Thank you. Stay for dinner. I'll just pop out to the store."

"I'll go with you," I said, getting to my feet, but she insisted she'd be fine on her own. I gave up and told her to take care out in the cold.

"What are you talking about? I'll only be gone five minutes!" Laughing, Mom wound her warm knitted scarf around her neck, pulled on her quilted overcoat and gloves, and set off.

Dinner that night was a feast of sukiyaki beef and vegetables. We rubbed the base of the cast-iron sukiyaki pot with fat until it melted, then threw in the meat, added the chopped vegetables, tofu, and *konnyaku* noodles, and seasoned the whole thing with soy sauce and sugar. We poured a little water over it, put on the lid, and let it simmer. When we took off the lid again, the steam that rose from the pot had a deliciously sweet aroma. Even though it was great to be sitting at the table surrounded by family, I couldn't help noticing that Mom had only bought cut-price beef, despite the ¥500,000 gift. Now I realized why she was so anxious to go shopping alone. She didn't want me to see how tight their household budget was.

My parents and Na-chan broke the raw egg into their bowls and beat it up with their chopsticks. They took big chunks of meat and tofu from the pot, dipped them in the egg, and wolfed them down hungrily. I ate my meat straight from the pot. I couldn't remember when we had last sat down to dinner together like this. It was a long time since I'd seen my parents' laughing faces and Na-chan's happy, childlike expression. These were simple things, but they made me happy. If only we had money, we could go back to those good times we used to have together.

Mom was suffering from high blood pressure, and had already collapsed twice, but she wasn't taking the medicine she'd been prescribed. She had no time for regular visits to the doctor, nor the money for the prescription. When I offered to pay for her doctor's visits, she would make excuses.

"I have to work, so I don't have time to go anyway," she'd say. Or, "If I collapse once more, then that'll be it for me. I don't need a doctor to tell me that."

I'd jokingly tell her not to say things like that, it'd bring her bad luck. I don't know if it was some kind of sixth sense that a daughter has about her mother, but I felt she didn't have much time left on this earth. Dad had recovered from his illness enough to live a fairly normal life again, but you couldn't really call him healthy, and if he got sick again it might be the end for him too. I was suddenly panicked by the feeling that time was running out for them. Mom never complained to anyone, but she did confide in me.

"Shoko-chan, your Dad and I are working as hard as we can so we can buy a little house for us all to live in. That's my dream, anyway."

It was my dream too. Maki and I had ruined our relationship with our parents by rebelling against them. Now that I'd finally managed to repair that relationship, I was determined never to risk it again. Somehow or other I was going to buy that house, and we would all live there together. I knew that there were heartless people who whispered behind my father's back that he had left the yakuza because he had been in so much trouble that he couldn't pay his dues, or that he had been a high-flier who had finally been brought down to earth, and other crap like that. Well, they didn't know the real facts of the story, and they knew nothing about Dad. Hearing people make fun of my family was incredibly painful. I vowed to myself that things wouldn't end this way—I'd find a way to turn things around.

I got back to my place, lit a cigarette, and sat there staring at the smoke as it curled up to the ceiling. The phone rang.

"Hello?"

"Shoko, I miss you."

"Shin! It's been forever! What's up?"

"I need to talk to you about something. Is it OK if I come over now?"

"Yeah, sure."

I hung up, wondering what could be so important that Shin couldn't tell me over the phone. When I heard the key in the door, I fetched us each a cup of coffee in cute matching mugs and sat down next to him.

"Talk to me."

"This is really hard for me to say... But I have to tell you."

"What?"

"My wife's pregnant."

"Um...congratulations." I somehow managed to give the appropriate response.

"Would you still want to see me if I had a kid?"

"What do you expect me to say?"

"I don't know, but I couldn't lie to you."

"I need to think it over." It was hard for me to meet his gaze.

"Are you mad at me?"

"No. But give me some time, OK?"

"I'll call you." He left without even touching his coffee.

Shin's wife pregnant... If I kept seeing Shin, and his wife found out, then I could be responsible for the breakup of a family. I knew ending it was the right thing to do, but I didn't want to lose him either. Now I had both Kuramochi's offer and Shin's news to think over. I had no idea what I was going to do.

Before I heard from Shin again, it was time for my date with Kuramochi. The minute I walked out of the apartment building, he leapt out of his car.

"Shoko! I missed you. I couldn't wait to see you again." He hugged me in full view of anyone who might be watching. I smelt the same scent as a week before when he'd kissed me. I couldn't remember when a man had hugged me so closely. His body felt warm against the winter chill.

"I missed you too," I said, meaning it.

"Really?"

"Yeah."

"Can I make love to you today?"

I nodded silently, my head resting on his shoulder. He took me back to his hotel. Once we were in the room, he hugged me again as tightly as before, then we fell onto the bed together. It was only the second time we'd met, but already it felt like we were soul mates. Still, I began to feel worried. I liked this man. I could really fall in love with him. I felt guilty about Shin, but I'd made up my mind not to go back to him.

"Where do you like to be touched?" I asked Kuramochi.

"Here," he answered, putting his hand to his chest, close to his heart.

I climbed on top of him, and began to gently lick his chest.

"That's enough," he said after a while, and caressing my breasts, he slipped his penis inside me. The sex was amazing. Even with Shin, I hadn't felt anything quite like this. Waves of pleasure washed over me again and again. Kuramochi seemed to be as overwhelmed as I was. Afterwards, he held my face in both hands and looked deep into my eyes. For no good reason at all, I suddenly felt embarrassed and my face began to burn.

"Hey, we've got great sexual chemistry, you and me. To think if we'd never made love we'd never have known," he said, grinning. Then his expression turned serious. "Shoko, you are the best lover I've ever had. Be my mistress. I'll take care of everything for you. This offer is for real—please think about it."

"Can you give me a little time?"

"You slept with me because you like me, right?"

"Of course. If I didn't like you I couldn't have."

"So what's the problem?"

"I just can't be with you right away."

"But you do want to be with me...?"

"I'm sorry... I just need to..."

"I see. You have other ties. I understand." He took out his wallet and produced a huge wad of cash. "Go on, take it." Like the last time, there was about ¥500,000.

"I don't need money," I said, trying to give it back to him.

"Oh, do I have to make you shut up again?" he demanded, pulling me to him and kissing me.

"If you keep doing that, I can't tell you what I'm thinking."

"Fine with me."

"Kuramochi-san, I'm sorry."

"There's no need to apologize. But next time I see you, you're coming back to Hirakata with me. And I'm going to have a house ready for you. Agreed?"

I thanked him for his offer, but I made no promises. He dropped me off at my apartment, and we talked on the phone again until he got home. When we finally hung up, I lay down on my bed to think, and my eye caught the apartment key lying beside me on the bedside table. What did that key mean to Shin? Thinking about him brought tears to my eyes. I wasn't lying to Kuramochi when I told him how much I liked him, but until I could sit down and talk to Shin I would never be able to sort out my feelings. There was one more thing that left me feeling depressed—if I had a relationship with Kuramochi it would be another affair. Why did I always fall in love with married men? I knew it was wrong, but I couldn't help it. Was I always going to be someone's lover? Was falling in love always so difficult? I knew I should break up with Shin now that I had begun an affair with Kuramochi, but I couldn't erase him from my heart just like that. All I had to do was choose Kuramochi and my parents would be able to start a new life. I was frustrated with myself for not being able to take that step.

At the same time that my parents were struggling with their debts, my sister Maki also had money problems. Her husband, Ogino, was a total loser and had never stuck with any job he started. On the surface, he seemed like an easygoing sort of guy, but the reality was completely different. One day, Maki came to see me.

"I really need to get a divorce, but I've no money and nowhere to live. I've put up with that deadbeat long enough."

"If you had somewhere to live, would you go ahead and do it?"

"Shoko, I'm desperate."

"OK, you can live here. I'll move somewhere nearby."

"You're not serious?"

"Yes. I'll go and see a real estate agent tomorrow and choose a place."

"Can I move my stuff in today? I don't think I can stand the sight of his face anymore."

"Sure, come right on over."

"You are awesome."

She didn't waste any time moving in. When she was done, she thanked me with such a look of pure relief on her face that I could see how hellish her situation had been. Maki and I spent the day together—the first in a very long time. And then, just like those long ago days when the two of us would sneak out to the disco, we spent the whole night talking and finally fell asleep on the same futon. The next day, I sublet Shin's apartment to my sister, and moved into a new place. Moving out should have been the perfect opportunity to break up with Shin, but I couldn't bring myself to end it. I even gave him a spare key to my new place.

There was an important reason I had chosen an apartment so close by.

Ogino had an obsessive, almost psychotic attachment to Maki, and had refused to listen to any talk of divorce. Maki had had to pack her things and get out of the house while he'd been out. Soon after she moved in, she started getting silent crank calls. I was pretty sure that at some point he'd try to force his way in, so I was ready to run over and help her at a moment's notice.

One evening, Maki and I were watching TV at her place when the crash of breaking glass behind us made us jump out of our skin. We turned to see Ogino climbing in through the window he had smashed. He grabbed Maki by the hair and started dragging her toward the door.

"Let go of her!" I screamed, kicking him as hard as I could.

"This is none of your fucking business," he shouted back, and punched me in the face.

"I'll kill you, you fucking asshole!" I could feel the blood pounding in my head. I leapt on him, and we began to kick and punch each other. Maki was in tears, begging him to stop. She tried to pull him off me, but she didn't have the strength.

"Maki, stay back!" I shouted, picking up the cassette player and hitting him over the head as hard as I could. He cried out in pain and curled up on the floor, holding his head. "If you really want to be rid of me that much, then go ahead, divorce me," he groaned.

"So you'll give her a divorce, then?" Blood trickled from my nose as I spoke.

"If she hates me that much!"

"Promise you'll never show your face around here again."

"No, I'll never bother either of you again." Ogino left the apartment looking totally crushed. The divorce became final a few days later, and Maki didn't waste any time in finding herself a job—as a bar hostess. It wasn't long before two of her clients asked her out. She couldn't decide which of them she liked, so she asked me to meet them both.

I went to meet the first one at a coffee shop near the bar where I worked. As I walked in, I heard Maki call out to me. I folded my coat neatly and placed it with my bag on the seat next to mine, then turned to the man sitting with my sister.

"I'm very pleased to meet you," I said, politely.

"It's a pleasure. My name's Takino."

The waitress arrived with a hot hand towel, and I ordered a coffee. I turned back to Maki and her friend and began to make conversation.

"What kind of work do you do, Takino-san?"

"I'm a chef."

"Yeah, Taki-kun's a chef and he's two years older than me." Maki leaned in closer to him. "Right?" she asked, nudging him in the ribs.

"You can call me Taki-kun too, if you like," he said to me. I got good vibes from him—he seemed like a really decent type.

Later he took us both home by taxi, and Maki called me as soon as she got in.

"What did you think of Taki-kun?"

"Seems like a good guy."

"He is. But I don't know... He's too serious for me."

"Well, I liked him."

"Wait till you meet the other guy. He's much cooler than Taki-kun."

I had a bad feeling about this. "What does the other guy do?"

"He doesn't work. He's from a rich family. And he buys me loads of stuff."

"So he's a typical playboy."

"No, he's not like that. He's smart too. He went to college."

"Being good at studying and being smart aren't the same thing."

"Huh. You're a total square sometimes, Shoko. But wait till you meet him. Then you'll get it. Can we get together tomorrow?"

"OK. Call me."

"Great. See you tomorrow."

"Night."

I hung up, thinking there was no point in even meeting him. These days, Maki carried a Chanel handbag, and all her clothes and accessories were brand name. I had a hunch now that these were presents from this other guy.

I turned up the next day at the family-style restaurant where we'd planned to meet. When I bowed and said, "Hello, it's nice to meet you," he laughed.

"Hey, Shoko, all that formal crap's so heavy. I hear about you from your sister all the time." He pushed the menu toward me. "Order whatever you want. Cool?"

"So, what's your name?"

"Yeah, they call me Itchan."

"It's a pleasure."

"Likewise."

He was certainly easygoing, and it looked like Maki was really into him. After talking for about an hour, we left the restaurant.

"I've got, like, an appointment, so I'll have to make tracks," announced Itchan, "Oh, here—for the taxi." He pushed ¥100,000 into Maki's hand.

"Thank you for dinner, Itchan," I said.

"Sure. Later, Shoko."

"Itchan, call me tomorrow," Maki called after him, waving madly. Then she turned to me.

"Well? He's a good guy, right?"

"I don't think you should see him."

"Why?"

"I'd stick with Taki-kun if I were you. Itchan'd make a good friend but I don't think he's dating material."

"Yeah…Taki-kun's a great guy too, and hardworking, so I've no complaints there, but I don't know—there's something missing. I get on better with Itchan."

"I can't lie to you, Maki. Please don't go there."

"What's wrong with him?"

"I think you'll end up hurt."

"You don't even know Itchan yet!"

"That's why I can see him for what he is."

Maki made a sulky face, then quickly changed the subject.

"So what about you?"

"What do you mean?"

"You've been with Shin-san forever now, but he's got a wife and you hardly ever get to see him. You never ever complain, so he thinks you're OK with the whole thing…"

"Maki!"

"I've been thinking this over for a long time, and I have to ask. Don't you have any feelings at all? You love Shin-san, don't you? How can you be so cool about it? There's no way he'll ever marry you. How can you be happy with that?"

"Don't change the subject. Aren't we supposed to be talking about you here?"

"I'm sorry. I just lost it for a sec. I shouldn't have said anything."

"That's OK. It's all true anyway. Look, don't be too hasty about those two guys. Why don't you think it over some more?"

"Yeah."

"And when you pick one of them, you'd better make sure you break it off completely with the other."

"I will. Anyway, thanks for coming today."

That evening when I got back to my apartment, Maki's words were echoing in my head.

Don't you have any feelings at all?

I really did have strong feelings for Shin. I wanted to hear him say, "I love you, Shoko," over and over, even if it wasn't true. But I was terrified that if I tried to put any kind of pressure on him, he'd stop loving me.

How can you be happy with that?

The answer to that question was that I wasn't ready to wake up from the dream and face reality yet. That was all I could tell myself right now.

Maki called me three days later. "I've broken up with Taki-kun." So she had chosen Itchan after all. "Itchan doesn't like me working nights, so I've quit the bar," she added.

Before long, Itchan moved in with Maki, but I felt uncomfortable with this arrangement at an apartment rented in Shin's name. Worse, Itchan was into gambling, and he thought nothing of betting hundreds of thousands of yen in a day. This was the "appointment" he had the first time we met. I warned Maki that gambling was like a disease that had no cure, and begged her to break up with him before he got into serious debt, but she just told me to chill out and stop being so small minded.

One day, shortly after Maki and Itchan got together, she came to me asking to borrow money. All I had to spare was that month's rent, which I had been about to pay—¥60,000. But I figured she must be desperate to come and ask me, so I lent her the whole ¥60,000.

"Shoko, I'm sorry. I really am. I'll call you later." Maki looked genuinely apologetic as she took it.

Then she and Itchan disappeared. It took me five days to realize it. I'd been trying to call Maki, but she never picked up. I suspected that they might have skipped town because of their debts, but I kept trying. Eventually, I got a recorded message from the phone company saying the line had been disconnected. I called the company and found that they owed ¥150,000. How in hell they managed to run up a bill like that, I had no idea. I was not only in total shock, but also in some serious shit. The phone was in Shin's name. If the phone company gave up billing him at the apartment and sent the bill to his home address instead, his wife would find out about me. I quickly arranged to have all bills transferred to my new address, and as it was too much for me to pay outright, I had them divide it into monthly installments.

Of course, Maki and Itchan were behind on the rent too. I went to apologize to the landlord and found him in a fury. "I've knocked on the door so many times, but no one ever answers. I reckon you've been pretending to be out." He slammed the rent book down on his desk. "I'll take what you owe me from your deposit. Just get out of the apartment!" I bowed as low as I could and apologized for all the trouble I'd caused, then ran to the apartment to clear out Maki's belongings. The electricity and water had been cut off, so the food in the refrigerator was rotten and stinking, and there was no way of washing my hands after touching it. I spent the whole day cleaning the place out. A secondhand store agreed to take all the furniture and household goods. When I'd finally sorted everything out, I went back to my own apartment, showered, and fell into bed, exhausted.

I hadn't been feeling good for several days. I put it down to stress and didn't worry too much. But one morning I felt nauseous for no particular reason and had to throw up. Surely it couldn't be...? I hurried to the drugstore and got myself a pregnancy test kit. Those days, people used to say that the more orgasmic the sex, the more likely you were to get pregnant, and I used to laugh at them, but my test result was positive. I'd got pregnant that time with Kuramochi. I didn't know what I was going to do, and I was too upset to contact him.

A few days later, I got a phone call from Maki.

"We're in Kyoto, and we're broke. We haven't eaten for two days. I'm starving, Shoko-chan. Please can you bring us some money?"

"OK. But I don't have very much to give you."

"Never mind. Just come, please."

I took some of my bags and jewelry to the pawnshop, and got on a train to Kyoto. Maki and Itchan were waiting on the platform at Kyoto Station and waved excitedly when they spotted me.

"Sorry!" Maki's long shaggy perm had been cut short, and she had put on a bit of weight. It had been a couple of months since I'd seen her, and I didn't recognize her right away.

"Hi, Shoko, sorry for the hassle. Let's go and hang in a café somewhere," said Itchan. He didn't sound the least bit sorry. The two of them really did look like they were starving as they put away several plates of pasta and pilaf. When they finally slowed down, I spoke to Maki.

"I was really worried. What happened to you?"

"I...uh, we..."

Itchan took over. "Sorry, Shoko, I fucked up."

"You've got gambling debts, haven't you?" I asked.

"Um, yeah. I couldn't stick around."

"So what are you going to do now?"

"Things'll work out," Itchan assured me. I sighed and massaged my forehead. "I'll take good care of Maki and the baby," he continued.

"What did you say? What baby?"

"I'm four months pregnant."

So that was why they hadn't eaten for two days, but Maki still looked fatter. Oh God, me and Maki both...

"Maki-chan, come home with me."

"No way! I'm not leaving Itchan."

"Why not?"

"I'm sorry, Shoko. I can't."

It was useless talking to her. I turned to Itchan.

"Itchan, please let Maki go."

"Shoko! What the hell?" gasped Maki.

"This is between me and Itchan," I said. "You shut up, Maki."

"Didn't I just tell you I'm not leaving him?"

"Hey, I know this is a real bummer, but I swear I'm gonna make Maki happy."

"How can you make her happy like this? Don't be so fucking irresponsible. If you care about Maki, let her go now."

Maki shook her head. "Shoko, I'm sorry. I'm not going with you."

"Oh, Maki-chan…"

Maki was a very tender and faithful person. There was no point in arguing any further, but I desperately wanted to take her home with me. On the other hand, it was Maki's life to live as she wanted.

"Look after yourself. If you ever need anything, call me. OK?"

"I will. Thanks, Shoko."

"Itchan, take care of Maki."

"Sure. Hey, thanks."

I left myself enough money to get home and handed the rest to Maki. Then I got out of Kyoto. I thought about Maki on the way back. She'd decided she was going to stay with Itchan and have the baby because she wanted to have the child of the man she loved. I realized that I felt the same way. Without having a clue how things would turn out, I'd subconsciously decided to have my baby. But I didn't plan to tell Kuramochi about it. I hadn't even called him once since we'd slept together, because I hadn't been able to make the break with Shin. To call him now, out of the blue, and tell him I was pregnant would only confuse him. I'd never given Kuramochi my new phone number. As long as I didn't call him, there was no way he could get in touch with me. I decided to tell Shin the truth. If I wanted to stay with him, then I had to tell him what had happened.

That was what I told myself anyway.

I needed money to pay off Maki's debts, cover my rent and living expenses, and to send to Mom and Dad, so I started working until four o'clock every morning. The hours were exhausting, but ever since I'd made up my mind to have the baby, it didn't seem to bother me so much. Now I understood those hostesses who used to bring my dad home—they were just trying to make a living. I quit smoking and began to eat a more balanced diet. I bought a bunch of baby name books and chose boy and girl names. I couldn't wait until my baby was born. Life was tough, but I was ecstatically happy.

My happiness was short lived. One morning I felt pains in my abdomen and I started to bleed. I rushed to the hospital, but it was too late. The high tension wire I'd been walking suddenly snapped. As I rubbed my empty belly, I imagined I was being punished for wanting to have the baby of a married man. Again, I had the feeling my grandpa was watching over me, and again I knew I had disappointed him. I called in sick to work, and went to bed. I spent the whole night crying.

I don't know what brought it on, stress or grief or what, but I ended up in the hospital with appendicitis. I'd had an inflamed appendix twice before, which had been cured with injections, but this time they had to operate, and they said I would be in the hospital for quite a long time. So I quit my job at the bar, went in for the operation, and spent two months there recovering, bored out of my skull.

My first night back at home, Shin turned up unexpectedly. As soon as I saw him, I ran and threw my arms around him.

"What happened to you? I've been out of my mind with worry."

"Appendicitis. They wouldn't let me out of the hospital. But I'm fine now."

"You could have paged me or something." I'd never called his pager. I was always afraid that his wife might be right there next to him. And no matter how much I might need to hear his voice, I'd promised myself that I would never ever pick up the phone and call him.

"I'm sorry."

"Well, I'm glad you're OK."

"Are you hungry? I could make us some dinner."

"That'd be great."

I'd only just got out of the hospital, so the refrigerator was almost empty except for a couple of salmon fillets in the freezer. I boiled some rice, made some miso soup, and defrosted the salmon, which I then sprinkled with salt and grilled.

"I'm sorry, this is all I've got."

"No, it tastes great."

"Good. You know, we've been together a long time, but this is the first time I've ever cooked you a meal."

Shin shifted uncomfortably. "Shoko, haven't you noticed I'm staying much later than usual?"

I was having such a good time I hadn't looked at the clock. "What is it? Has something happened?"

"My wife's in the hospital."

"Huh?"

"She had the baby."

Somehow I managed to smile and congratulate him, but so many thoughts were racing around in my mind, and it felt as if something was blocking my throat. This was reality—I had to accept that I wasn't the most important thing in Shin's life. His family came first, and it was time for me to end things with him.

"I think we should break up." I'd finally managed to say it.

"Don't be mad at me, Shoko."

"Go and be a good father."

"Do you mean that?"

"I can't see you anymore." I looked down at the floor. If I looked at Shin's face, I'd be in danger of changing my mind.

"It's up to you. I always hoped we'd be able to spend one whole night together, but I guess that's not going to happen now." He put his key down on the dining table and stood up. "I won't be here to say it, so, happy twentieth birthday, Shoko."

He went straight to the front door, and for a moment his hand seemed to pause on the door handle, but then he opened it. The door shut with a heavy, hollow sound, and he was gone.

Three years from my seventeenth to my twentieth birthday sounds like a long time, but it was far too short. To put it simply, I loved Shin and wanted to spend more time with him. He was someone who was always just beyond my reach, but who never abandoned me either. After three years of being with a man like Shin, I was really afraid of being on my own.

CHAPTER SIX

Tattoo

The rainy season came around again. I used to sit staring out of my window at the hydrangeas in the yard of the little house next door, watching the raindrops slide off the petals like tears. The sky was grey and gloomy and reflected my mood exactly.

I responded to an ad for a hostess and started working again. At the new place, I had a client called Ito, a yakuza about ten years older than me, who was very sweet. He was the kind of person who got along with everybody and was always attentive, but he seemed to have a special thing for me, and after a time he tried to persuade me to date him.

"Will you go out with me? I'm single. I'm not playing around."

I was still thinking about Kuramochi, and I couldn't give Ito a clear answer.

One day after work, I met Ito at another bar near my workplace. He introduced me to the *mama-san*.

"This is one of the girls who works at Noriko's place. Her name's Shoko."

"Pleased to meet you." I said, with a slight bow.

"Is that right? I know your boss real well. She's a great mama-san. Such a hard worker, and a looker too!"

Grinning, she exchanged Ito's ashtray for a clean one.

"Hey, Mama, I really like this girl, but she won't go out with me. Won't you talk to her for me?"

"Shoko-chan, Ito-san's a good man. And he's single. Take my word for it. I live in his neighborhood. I run into him all the time in the convenience store buying beer, and he's always alone."

"Yeah, that's right, you always catch me when I'm dressed like a bum…"

"Yes, and me without any makeup on too!" The owner made a face like *The Scream*, and the two of them giggled. Obviously Ito was a regular here. Still, I didn't give him an answer that day either.

A few days later, I got the flu and had to take the night off. I was fast asleep when I was woken by the sound of the doorbell. I reached out to look at my watch on the bedside table and saw that it was a little after nine o'clock.

"Yes?" I called through the front door.

"Shoko, it's me. Ito."

"Ito-san? What are you doing here?"

I opened the door. It turned out Ito had called the bar and been told I'd taken the day off. Worried, he'd called a friend of mine and heard that I was sick in bed. He'd come over to bring me a gift—an expensive variety of melon.

"A get-well present. Hope you like fruit."

"I do. Thanks."

"Have you eaten?"

"Not really. I've been asleep all day."

"What? Hey, you gotta eat to get better. What you need is some rice gruel. Mind if I use your kitchen?"

"No, but…"

"Just relax. Won't take me long."

He wasted no time pulling off his jacket and rolling up his sleeves.

Then, kind of awkwardly, he began to prepare the gruel. It was clear he wasn't used to being in the kitchen.

"I'm not much of a cook, so it might not taste great." He flashed me a charming smile.

After a while, he announced it was ready. I struggled to my feet, but I got dizzy all of a sudden and almost fainted.

"Wait, don't move," Ito ordered, then he scooped me up in his arms and carried me to my chair. I weakly managed to lift the spoon to my mouth.

"It's good."

"You're not just saying that?"

"No, it's delicious."

"Well, that makes it all worthwhile." He looked so pleased I couldn't help smiling. When I'd finished eating, he picked me up as easily as before and took me back to bed. He spent the whole night next to me, holding my hand. It reminded me of when I was little and used to get sick. Mom would sit at my bedside watching over me all night. I don't know if it was the fever or what, but I even imagined Ito's rice gruel tasted the same as hers. I felt safe with Ito's big warm hand holding mine.

"I'm serious about you, Shoko. Would you ever think about marrying me someday?" It was the first thing he said to me when I woke up the next morning. His eyes were pleading. I knew a man like this would never let me down.

"Yeah, maybe I could."

"Really? No kidding?" He was so psyched that he punched the air, and the smile on his face was like a little kid's. This time I laughed along with him.

I didn't know much about Ito yet. But perhaps I should have noticed that he had the same tattoo on his back as Maejima.

A few months later, someone told me the unthinkable. Ito was already married, and I was just his lover. The news hit me like a ton of bricks. I had suspected he might have another girlfriend somewhere, but never that he was hiding a wife from me. That night I tried to end it.

"You're married, you bullshitter!"

"What are you talking about? Me, married?"

"How long were you planning to hide it from me? Well, that's it. I don't want to see you anymore."

"Calm down a minute. I know I shouldn't have lied to you, but if I'd told you the truth, you wouldn't have gone out with me. I didn't mean to cheat. I was going to tell you eventually... I'm sorry. Please don't end it, Shoko-chan, I'm begging you."

"I don't know." I had really begun to care about Ito, but what could I say?

"I don't want to break up. You've got to understand. I know I was wrong." He threw his arms around me and hugged me as if he was afraid I'd leave there and then. "I love you. You're the only woman I want." He started to cry. Hearing these words and seeing a man cry got me all choked up.

"I know... I feel the same way about you, but..."

That was my problem—I was always too quick to forgive people and too much of a wimp to stand up for myself against men. In the end, I gave in, and accepted the role of lover yet again.

It wasn't long before I began to notice some changes in Ito's behavior. He would stay at my apartment almost every night, but if he was ever busy, he'd tell one of the younger mobsters from his gang to pick me up from work and bring me home. He'd call me on the phone as many as twenty or thirty times a day. He had a spare key and would often let himself in when I wasn't there and push the redial button on my phone to find out the last number I'd called. If it connected him to one of my friend's houses, he'd ask if I was there, and when I came on the line, he'd tell me to hurry up and get home. Then he'd keep on calling to see if I'd left yet, so I could never relax, and in the end had to give up visiting with friends.

One time, the last number I'd called turned out to be a taxi company. He asked them what time they'd picked me up and where they'd taken me. When I got home, he innocently asked me where I'd been. I'd had it with him getting on my case, so I shrugged and told him I'd been out with friends. Suddenly his tone changed. "What kind of friends? Where do you know them from?" It felt like a police interrogation. I couldn't stand it anymore.

"It's none of your business!"

"So you're seeing someone behind my back!" He leapt up and hit me in the face.

"What the fuck?" I lost my temper and hit him back, but then he kicked me in the stomach. The force made me stumble backward, sending kitchen utensils clattering to the floor. Ito took a heavy mug and smashed it over my head. Blood began to drip onto the kitchen mat. He swung me around by the hair, and I heard a kind of ripping sound as a chunk of skin peeled away from my scalp. He punched me until my top front teeth were knocked crooked and one of the bottom ones fell out. There was a cracking sound from my nose and one eyelid began to swell. Then I stepped on a piece of the broken mug and, with a moan of pain, collapsed on the floor. After I'd lain there a while, Ito reached down and hugged me right there on the blood-soaked floor.

"Shoko, I'm sorry. I love you. Please forgive me."

But Ito's behavior only continued to get worse, and word of it even got back to some of the other yakuza in his gang. One higher ranking yakuza, called Otsuka, couldn't bear to stand back and watch what Ito was doing, and he took it on himself to help me. He'd tell Ito to end it with me, that being obsessed with a woman this way was no example for the young guys in the gang. He'd point out how much Ito owed to his wife. It seemed she had supported him a lot in the past, and had played a large role in helping him rise quickly through the ranks. But Ito told him that it wasn't anybody's business but his own, and refused to listen to any advice.

Otsuka got sick of trying. He'd tell me, "One of these days he's going to kill you. The guy's out of his mind. I wish I could help, but I don't know what else to do."

Ito would get all worked up and tell me he was never going to let me go, and his violent attacks were happening more frequently. When he was done hitting me, he would start crying and say something like, "Shoko, I feel terrible. Please forgive me. It's you, you drive me crazy. I've never felt this way about anyone before. Shoko, promise me you'll never leave me. I'm begging you…" He would look at me with big doggy eyes, like our old family pet. I even felt sorry for him, worried that if I left him, he'd be lonely.

Otsuka told me Ito used to be a different guy. "Before you, he was a regular playboy. He got bored of women real quick. His wife was the only one he ever cared about. I don't know what's happened to him. He's pathetic these days."

Ito always had excuses for the way he treated me. To Otsuka he'd complain, "I love Shoko so much, but she's always trying to leave me. What else can I do?" And to me, "Why can't you understand how I feel? When you tell me you want to break up, it makes me so mad I just act out. Afterwards I know it was wrong, but I can't control myself."

It was impossible to make sense of this distorted, obsessive thing that he called love. I was sick of hearing the same old phrases day in and day out, like an irritating broken record. Gradually, my feelings for him began to change.

One evening, I got a call at work from Otsuka.

"There's someone I want you to meet. Don't let Ito know. Make sure you meet me after work. Got it?" he said urgently. I hadn't a clue who it might be.

When I got to the meeting place, I took one look at Otsuka's mystery guest and was blown away. It was Kuramochi.

I sat there in a daze for a while, until Kuramochi finally spoke.

"Shoko, Otsuka-san told me everything. I can't believe what you're going through. Why didn't you call me?"

I couldn't answer.

"It's my fault. I should have got in touch with you earlier. If only I'd taken you back with me that night, none of this would have happened."

"It's not your fault. I'm sorry I didn't call you, but it's difficult to explain to people about this kind of thing."

"I'm not 'people'. You know I'd do anything for you. Well, there's no need to worry anymore. Come on, I'm taking you home."

Otsuka explained that he had been meeting a business associate earlier that day, and the other guy had turned up with Kuramochi. Otsuka and Kuramochi had hit it off and soon realized that they both knew me. Otsuka had told him what was going on with Ito, and Kuramochi had immediately decided to come and rescue me. He'd asked Otsuka to settle things with Ito for him and offered to pay him a ¥5 million reward for sorting it out. The reason I hadn't heard from Kuramochi for so long was that shortly after the last time we'd met, his business had gone through a rough patch and he'd had to concentrate on crisis management. When he'd finally got through the worst of it, he called, but found my number out of use. He guessed I'd found myself somebody else, so he'd tried to forget about me. It turned out he couldn't. After hearing Kuramochi's story, Otsuka thought he'd found a way at last to save me from Ito.

It was amazing to hear that Kuramochi was still interested in me, and mind-blowing that after all this, he still wanted to me to be his lover. I felt flattered and excited. But another thought was eating away at me—the ¥5 million. It was like blood money. I was being bought. How had it come to this? Did Kuramochi really care about me? Or had he always seen me as goods to be paid for? And what would Ito do when he found out I'd run away with Kuramochi? He'd be a laughing stock in his gang. Even if Otsuka could sort things out with him, he'd think he'd been betrayed for money, and was sure to hold a grudge.

"Shoko, I told Kuramochi-san I didn't want any money, but he's insisting. He's a real old-fashioned gent—not too many of those around these days. To be honest with you, I think you should go with him right now. If you don't, you'll never get away from Ito. And it'll be for that dumbshit's own good too. He's screwing one of the girls from Masae's bar too, you know. He thinks he's such a stud. In the office, we're always laughing at him behind his back."

She has to take responsibility for her own actions. My father's words snuck into my head. I made a decision. I turned to Kuramochi. "I'm really happy that you feel this way about me, but I can't go with you."

"What?" Both men looked at me in amazement.

"Good night," I said, half to myself, stood up, and bowed my head to them.

"Hey, are you going to be OK going home by yourself?"

"Ito won't be there today. Anyway, I'll be fine." With this lie, I started to leave, but Kuramochi caught me by the hand. "We'll wait for another hour, in case you change your mind." I couldn't look him in the eye. I ran as fast as I could toward the exit.

By the time I got home, I had psyched myself up for what I knew was going to happen. As soon as I got through the apartment door, Ito grabbed the front of my blouse and got right in my face.

"Hey, you've been out with Otsuka tonight, haven't you? I heard from Ishimoto. What did the two of you have to talk about? Tell me!"

The two of you... So he didn't know about Kuramochi.

"I wasn't with Otsuka," I blurted.

"What the fuck? What d'you mean you weren't with him?"

"And you and I are through. I heard you've got another woman. Looks like you've had enough of me. Because you know, I'm totally sick and tired of you."

"That woman? She doesn't mean anything to me. I'll break it off with her. But I'm not letting you finish with me. No fucking way!" He picked up a beer bottle and swung it at my head.

"Go on! Hit me as much as you like!"

"What did you say?"

"Go ahead, hit me again."

"Yeah? You want more?" He kicked me in the chest and I flew backward, landing on my back on the floor. He kept on pummeling me. Blood came from my ear, I felt my nose break yet again, and my false tooth flew out of my mouth. There was so much blood in my throat that I was almost choking. Ito pinned me to the floor with one foot, so he could kick me more easily with the other. I remember hearing a loud ringing in my ears, and then I must have passed out.

"Hey, Shoko! Come on! Shoko?"

I heard Ito's voice and cracked open one swollen eyelid to see his face, white as a sheet, hovering over me.

"I'm so sorry. Forgive me, Shoko-chan."

The same old bullshit. I summoned my strength to shout, "Get out!"

"Shoko..."

"Leave me alone!"

"I'm really, really sorry." Ito sulkily left the apartment, looking like a kid who'd been told off by his parents. Somehow I dragged myself to my feet, and got myself to the ER at the hospital down the street. The doctor wanted to admit me, but I only agreed to be an outpatient. I got fixed up and returned home.

The next morning, Otsuka called.

"I heard from Ito what happened. I don't get it. How could you let him almost beat you to death like that? What were you thinking? I told you I'd take care of it for you."

"I'm sorry. Believe me I am sorry. And please tell Kuramochi-san not to call me anymore."

"I'll talk to Kuramochi-san, but please think about it. You'd be saving yourself."

"Otsuka-san, thank you for everything, but I can't see Kuramochi-san again."

"Are you sure?"

"I'll call and tell him myself."

"You'll regret it."

"I will end it with Ito. I just need a little time. I'm sorry for all the trouble I've caused you." I hung up the phone.

So long, Kuramochi.

This time it really was the final good-bye.

It was right after this that I made a life-changing decision. One Sunday afternoon, I was out shopping when I ran into my old friend Yukie.

"Shoko, do you have a minute?"

"Sure. What's up?"

"My boyfriend just called me—he's getting a tattoo. He's almost done, so I told him I'd go and wait for him. Thing is, I'm nervous about going there by myself..."

"No problem, but it's not like you're going alone. Your boyfriend's there already, right?"

"Yeah, but it looks so painful. I don't think I can even bear to sit in there by myself."

"There's no problem me coming?"

"No problem at all. It's right near here too. Come on."

So we set off for the tattoo parlor. One of the apprentice tattoo artists welcomed us and led us to a waiting lounge with a couch. I opened one of the albums on the table, and looked at photos of what must have been the tattoo master's work. One in particular caught my eye. It wasn't just a tattoo: it was a piece of art using the human body as a canvas, with delicately curving lines representing graceful koi leaping up a foaming waterfall. I'd grown up surrounded by men with tattoos, starting with my father, and I'd never felt there was anything wrong with having one. Ever since I was a kid I'd loved to draw, and I was sure I'd been inspired by the beautiful work of art on my father's body. But nothing had ever spoken to me like the work of this tattoo master.

"Let's get out of here." Yukie's boyfriend appeared with the tattoo master. Yukie introduced me.

"Sensei, this is my friend Shoko."

"Pleased to meet you."

The tattoo master was an older man with twinkling eyes and a serene smile.

"Awesome! Shoko, look."

Yukie had lifted up her boyfriend's shirt to look at his brand new tattoo. His skin was swollen and bleeding slightly, and looked pretty sore, but in return he had been given something of indescribable beauty. That was when I made up my mind.

"Sensei, I'd like you to do one for me too."

"You're not serious?" Yukie was shocked.

"Sure I am. I want this artist to do my tattoo."

"No point in talking to you once you've made up your mind. Well, we've gotta get going. Later!"

"Sorry," I said, joining my hands in a humble gesture of apology. Yukie laughed and waved to me from the door. I turned back to the tattoo master.

"So, could you?"

"Of course. The minute I saw you, I thought you'd look great with a tattoo, but I'm not allowed to suggest it."

"Really?"

"I've got the perfect one. It's uniquely you."

"I'd like to see it."

He opened a drawer filled with tattoo designs, pulled one out, and laid it on the table for me to see.

"This is Jigoku Dayu. She was a courtesan in the Muromachi era. She was a real person, and she lived right here in Sakai. These women lived in the pleasure quarters, and they could either work until they'd paid off their purchase price, or try to catch the eye of a patron and have their freedom paid for. It was a tough life."

"Why did you think of her?"

"How can I explain...? It was just the feeling I got from you. And in this image, Dayu has so many different hair accessories. This means she was the number one courtesan in the pleasure quarter."

I had always wanted to be someone's number one, but always ended up being number two. The men in my life were always telling me they loved me, but I never thought I was good enough for them. Because of my lack of self-confidence, if someone told me they loved me, I was content to hang back and let them take the lead, and that was how I ended up drifting along in relationships with married men. I let them get away with murder. Well, that was it for me—no more wimpy attitude. It was time to start over.

"I'll have this one."

"Don't you want to see any of the other designs?"

"No."

"So it's a deal then?"

I gave him a decisive nod, scheduled my appointments, and left the tattoo parlor. When I got home, I took a bath and examined my back in detail in the bathroom mirror. This tattoo would be for myself and no one else. It wasn't just because I was about to end my relationship with Ito, it was because I wanted to make some serious changes deep down inside me.

The next Friday, I put on some old clothes that I didn't mind getting messed up and went to the tattoo parlor. I had originally planned just to have my torso done, but in the end I decided to add a dragon to each arm. We got started right away. First, the outline had to be drawn on the skin. The burning pain of the machine's tiny pulses moving back and forward over the same lines made me feel as if I was being cut with a broken razor blade. The session took three hours.

"That's enough for today," said the master, turning off the machine. I paid and hurried home, quickly changed my clothes, and headed off to work.

Because of the master's schedule, I had to visit him every day for about the same length of time. I'd been going to the tattoo parlor for several days when I met up with Otsuka to let him know I was ending it with Ito.

"He's still with that other woman, so it's probably a good idea," he agreed.

I moved in quickly on Ito. He starting bluffing like before, telling me he'd break up with the other woman right away, but as he'd been cheating the whole time he'd been with me anyway, no excuse was going to cut it. He did hit me at one point, but I was used to that now. It didn't matter how much he raged or what he did, I stood my ground. In the end, Ito realized I wasn't going to back down, and handed over my spare key.

And finally, my tattoo was finished too. My torso—back and front—and my shoulders, breasts, and upper arms were decorated with a vibrantly colored work of art. I knew it had been the right thing to do.

While the tattoo was fresh, the blood would ooze out and stick to my shirt, and I had to be very careful not to peel off any skin when I got undressed. When I got into a hot bath, I would sting all over. To make sure it didn't get infected or scab over, I rubbed in anti-inflammatory ointment every spare moment I had. Over time, the sting faded, but next it started to itch like crazy, and peel as if I'd had a bad sunburn. I was desperate to scratch it, but there was no way I'd risk damaging it, so I somehow managed to stop myself. Eventually the itching calmed down. When I looked at that beautifully crafted tattoo, I was filled with a sense of total contentment I had never experienced before. I felt as though I had been set free.

CHAPTER SEVEN

Clean Break

Since getting the tattoo, my attitude to work had changed. Before, I'd gone to work because I had to, and had wandered fairly aimlessly through life. Now I was beginning to take things more seriously and found a new kind of enthusiasm, both for work and for life. That was when I met Takamitsu, a yakuza four years older than me. It was one night when I had gone out drinking with a group of clients.

"Takamitsu. What an unusual name. Sounds kind of old fashioned."

"Actually, it's my family name."

"Oh? I thought it was your first name. Sorry."

"It's nothing to be sorry about. People are always getting it wrong."

"And everyone calls you Taka for short, right?"

"Right. So why don't you call me Taka too?"

He laughed, and in that moment everything around him froze, and Taka seemed to be the only person alive. It wasn't long before he asked me out, but I'd taken so much shit from the string of men I'd dated that I was pretty nervous about getting involved with a new guy. I didn't give him an answer, but over time I did tell him the truth about everything that I'd been through. Taka wasn't put off at all, and we began to meet up regularly in the daytime. We'd go to movies, eat lunch, go for a drive together, and he'd even take me shopping for clothes or shoes. Sometimes when I felt miserable, he'd just sit quietly by my side. He was a warm and caring person.

One time, I was out with him in the car when he suddenly said, "Didn't you use to live around here? Which way is it?" He began to head toward my old family house, which of course we no longer owned.

"I don't want to go anywhere near it!"

"How long are you planning to live in the past? You've got to try to move on." It was the first time Taka had ever raised his voice to me. It was as if he could see into the dark corners of my mind. I couldn't say a thing, except direct him to the house.

"Turn left over there."

We stopped in front of the house and got out. I instinctively reached out to open the gate, but it was securely locked. I wondered how the koi were doing—were they being properly fed? And there was the old cherry tree. I longed to touch it once more. But I couldn't reach it from out here.

Once, when I was a kid, Mom had told me, "You were the apple of your grandpa's eye. He absolutely doted on you."

"That's right," Dad had added. "He was always talking about you. This is for you to remember him by." He took something from a drawer and put it in my hand. It was Grandpa's old pocket watch, and it felt like his heart beating there in the palm of my hand. But over the years it began to lose time and eventually stopped. My life until now was like grandpa's pocket watch. Somewhere along the way, I had started to lose a grip on time. I'd wasted so much of the time I'd lived in this house and then spent so long wishing I could get it back. I hated that the home Dad had built for our family now belonged to strangers. But I couldn't forget that it held a bunch of unpleasant memories for me too. The years I had lived there, it was as if my mind and body had been in different places. I had ended up losing touch with myself. And here I was, so tied up in the past that I was unable to move forward. Why was I avoiding the present?

"Enough with the self-pity, already! You've got a good man here," I told myself.

"Will you marry me?" Right there in front of the iron gate, in sight of the cherry tree, Taka slipped a Tiffany ring onto my finger. He'd caught me completely off guard with his proposal, but I looked him straight in the eyes and told him yes. A breeze rippled through the branches of the cherry tree. It felt like good-bye.

"Do you think I should ask your parents' permission?"

"Yes. Let's do it now."

I leaned toward the cherry tree and whispered good-bye. As we drove away from the house I'd grown up in, I never even glanced back. I kept my eyes straight ahead, looking into the bright sunshine.

Would Dad be against the marriage? I worried all the way from the car, through the front door, and into the living room.

"Dad, I need to talk to you about something important. Have you got a minute?"

"Of course. What is it?" My father put down the newspaper he was reading. Taka came straight to the point.

"My name is Takamitsu. It's a pleasure to meet you. I'd like your permission to marry Shoko."

Without batting an eye, Dad asked, "What line of work are you in?"

"I'm a member of the Ose-gumi syndicate."

"Yes, I know the boss well. Hmm. I see..." Mom and I sat there nervously as Dad continued. "Fine. Takamitsu, you'd better make my daughter very happy."

I couldn't believe Dad had taken to him right off.

"I will," answered Taka.

"Shoko-chan, congratulations! I'm so happy for you," said Mom, a look of relief on her face. Dad and Taka talked for a while, then we went back to my apartment.

That night in bed, Taka gently took off all my clothes. It was the first time I'd ever shown my tattoo to a man, and I was really nervous, but Taka stroked my back and told me it was beautiful.

"Thank you."

I closed my eyes and put my arms around him. There was something familiar about sex with Taka, as if finally my mind and body had been reunited.

As Taka's dragon and lion tattoo entwined itself around my Dayu, I imagined how happy the courtesan must have been to have found her patron at last. I slept deeply until morning, and the first thing I did when I opened my eyes was to put my arms around him and pull him toward me again.

"Shoko..." He mumbled my name sleepily.

We made love again and it was as good as the night before, then I went back to sleep with my head on his shoulder.

We had my parents' blessing, but there were people in Taka's life who knew about Ito and his obsessive attachment to me. They told Taka I was going to be trouble and warned him to stay away from me, but Taka always told them he'd never leave me. They'd warn him I was too much to handle, and to get the hell out of it while he still could. When I heard about things like this, I was choked with fear that he might leave me, but Taka had made a commitment and he had gone into it with his eyes wide open.

I promised myself I'd never cause this guy any pain. But I spent many sleepless nights worrying that Ito would show up again. And then it happened.

One morning, Taka had gone to the jail to take part in a traditional yakuza welcome for some gang member who was being released. Ito must have been waiting for me on the staircase landing. He ran up behind me as I was heading out with the garbage.

"Hey! So you think you're marrying that Takamitsu from the Osegumi gang? The fuck you are!"

He grabbed me by the hair and began to bang my head relentlessly against the concrete wall.

"You and I are finished. It's none of your business anymore!" Blood was pouring from my head down my neck, and I was fighting to stay conscious.

"You belong to me!"

"Get over it!"

Next thing, all I saw was the shiny black leather of his shoe heading for my face. He continued kicking me for what seemed like forever, then picked up the plant on the landing, pot and all, and shattered the whole thing over my head. I fell onto the broken pieces, and he kept punching and kicking me as I lay there covered in dirt. By now, I couldn't even feel the pain. I'd been beaten so hard that I didn't have the strength left to raise a hand to protect myself. Suddenly, Ito seemed to snap out of his frenzy and the punches stopped.

"Shoko, let's get back together," he said, dragging me into the apartment and pushing me onto the bed.

"Please, Ito-san, don't!"

"Shut up, or I'll kill you!" He punched me in the face again and tore off my clothes, climbed on top of me, and using his saliva to make me wet, forced his penis inside me. That moment of penetration released a flood of horrible memories. I was back in my bedroom as a child, being assaulted by Mizuguchi.

"Shoko, make some noise. Show me how much you like it."

The very same words used by that lowlife Maejima, and the very same kabuki tattoo pounding away on top of me...

"Feels good, doesn't it? I'm so much better than Taka, aren't I? Hey, move your hips a bit. It'll feel even better."

He still had hold of my hair and was panting like a dog. The sweat poured from his face onto my forehead, rolled down my temples, and dripped onto the sheets.

This is nothing. It's just sex. It doesn't mean anything.

I bit my split lip as hard as I could. From my tightly shut eyes the tears began to roll, mixed with blood, and reminding me again of the bad old days with Maejima. Ito's hand had held mine for that whole night when I was sick. I remembered how warm and comforting it had been. Now it was repulsive to me...

"Shoko, I'm taking you to the hospital."

I couldn't move, so Ito picked me up and carried me to his car. When we arrived at the hospital, he brought me into the consultation room himself. With a single glance, the doctor knew that I'd been beaten up. He turned to Ito and very suspiciously asked him what had happened.

"She fell down the stairs."

"Fell? All these serious injuries to her face, were they just from a fall?"

"Ah, yes, when she fell she hit the corner of a table. Then, um, well..."

Ito was clearly flustered. He knew he was on dangerous ground. But if he was going to be arrested, surely the doctor would have called the police right away...

I couldn't stand Ito being there any more. "Get the hell out of here! I never want to see your face again!" I shouted, with as much energy as I had left in my broken body. For a moment, he looked uncomfortable. He made his way to the door. But as he left, he flashed me a warning look.

The doctor began to take a close look at my injuries. My left arm, left hand, right kneecap, and two ribs were all broken. My nose was fractured, my left eyelid and right upper lip were cut, and there were two deep cuts in my head.

"Tendo-san, the places on your head that we have to sew up will be hidden by your hair, but your face will be scarred. I don't think the other injuries will completely heal either."

I'm going to be permanently scarred...

"Go ahead and sew me up. I don't want any anesthetic."

The doctor nearly fell over. "Without anesthetic? It'll hurt too much. You won't be able to stand the pain."

"Doctor, you can see how much pain I've already put up with. Please do what I'm asking."

The doctor saw that I meant it, and sighed. He didn't say a word throughout the operation. Finally, he spoke.

"Tendo-san, I'm finished. Now try not to get too depressed about all this."

"Thank you very much." I bowed deeply.

On my way out, I picked up my prescription, and returned home with my left arm in a plaster cast. I turned the key in the lock, but the door was already open. Taka was home.

"Hey, what the fuck has been going on in here?" yelled Taka from inside. Blood was splattered on the walls, and the place was turned upside down.

"Really, it wasn't that bad," I answered.

Taka took one look at me, and his face turned purple with rage.

"Ito, wasn't it?"

He went to the closet where he kept his .38 caliber revolver, put three bullets into it, and headed for the door.

"Taka, where are you going with that? Wait! Please wait!"

"Shut up!"

I caught hold of his sleeve, but he pushed my hand away. He tucked the gun into his waistband and left, slamming the door behind him. I ran to the phone and called one of the senior members of his gang.

"Please stop Taka. He's going to kill Ito!"

"Shoko? What's going on? Slow down. I can't understand a word you're saying."

I summed it up as quickly as I could.

"The dumbfuck..." He must have dropped the receiver because I could hear him hollering, "Someone go and get Takamitsu now! Bring him back here!"

"Hello? Are you still there?"

"Shoko, don't move from your apartment. Got it?"

I was panicked, but there was nothing to do but sit and wait for Taka to come home. Night had fallen by the time he turned up, a bandage wrapped around his left hand.

"Taka!"

"You called my boss didn't you? He told me not to do something stupid over a woman, but how could I live with myself if I didn't? So I beat that little shit Ito to a pulp, and I told the boss I'm quitting."

I knew what that meant in the yakuza world. My eyes moved to his left hand. I realized now where the blood on the bandage was coming from. He had cut off his little finger.

"Oh my God."

"I had to do it. I can't be a yakuza if it means letting someone get away with doing this to my woman. No one makes a fool of a yakuza. It's over."

"I'm sorry. I really am. I'm so sorry."

"Why are you apologizing?"

"Because it's all my fault."

"It's not your fault. Stop crying."

I couldn't tell him now that Ito had raped me. All I could do was beg him to forgive me.

"Shoko...Shoko... Don't worry about it."

"Make love to me."

"How can we, with you in that state?"

"Please."

"When you're better."

"Do it now."

"It'll hurt."

I wanted to tell him that my heart was hurting far more than any physical injuries.

"Did something else happen today?" asked Taka.

"No..."

"Shoko, are you hiding something from me?"

"No, I swear it's nothing."

"OK, Let's get married tomorrow."

"Tomorrow?"

"It's your birthday, right?"

"You remembered?"

"Of course."

"Let's go stay with Maki. Start over, just the two of us."

The next day we went to the city office and registered our marriage. For my birthday I got a new name—Shoko Takamitsu. I gave up my apartment, and with nothing but a small amount of cash and one overnight bag, Taka and I left Osaka for good.

Maki and Itchan had moved from Kyoto and were renting an apartment in Yokohama. As I sat in the bullet train, I went over all the events of the previous day and felt nothing but pain—physical and emotional. How could I have loved someone who punched and kicked me like that? I thought I had explained my feelings to him. I hadn't felt any hate for him or held a grudge since we'd split up. So why did he? Why did he have to make me suffer right to the end?

The memory of Ito's sweat dripping on my forehead, and his hot, clammy body gave me gooseflesh. I had no affection left for the city where I'd been born and brought up.

We arrived at Maki's place in Yokohama. Their apartment was in a dilapidated old wooden building. Our footsteps clattered on the flimsy metal staircase that led up to the second floor. We rang the bell and Maki opened the door.

"Hi! Come on in!"

The apartment was small, just two rooms divided by paper sliding doors. In the smaller room there was a kotatsu table up against the wall and a TV set on top of some cheap wooden storage shelves. The TV was playing a candy commercial with a bunch of cartoon characters dancing in a row. Bears or rabbits or something.

"Shoko, look at you! You'd better take it easy for a while."

"No, I don't have the time for that. Do you know of any work around here?"

"Well...," said Maki dubiously, glancing at Taka's left hand. Then Itchan spoke up.

"Leave it to me. I know a dude who manages a pachinko parlor. He's looking for staff. I'll put a word in for you."

"Thanks, that'd be cool." I put my hand on Taka's knee. "We really don't have much cash. We'll be in the shit if we don't get jobs quickly."

At that moment, our joint finances added up to less than ¥10,000, so Taka was quick to agree.

Itchan called up the pachinko parlor and we got interviews right away. He also handed us a sports newspaper with the horse racing section marked here and there with red ink. I hadn't exactly been hopeful, but it was clear he hadn't kicked his gambling habit.

It took a train and a bus to get to the pachinko parlor to meet Hara, the manager. After we explained our circumstances and asked if we could use an employee apartment, he agreed, and said I could take the first month to recuperate. We arranged that I would help out with some simple office work until my face healed and my arm came out of the cast, and then move to the service counter. Taka would start right away working as a floor attendant.

In the beginning, we were dirt poor. The month before our first paychecks arrived, we avoided spending money by recycling everything, including plastic vending machine cups. On the way to work, we passed a house that was being knocked down, and in the debris, we found a square piece of mirror. We took it home and set it on top of piles of old magazines, creating an instant dressing table. The edges of the mirror had started turning black, and the glass was cloudy, so the faces reflected back at us seemed to be shrouded in mist. But it didn't matter how tough things were because the only thing we cared about was working as hard as we could.

One day I began to lift a crate of canned drinks when I felt a sharp pain in my abdomen and noticed I was bleeding. I got permission from Hara to leave, and went straight to the hospital.

"Takamitsu-san, you're starting to miscarry. You need complete bed rest," said the doctor.

I was blown away by the news that I was pregnant, but there was no way I could afford to take it easy right now. We were only allowed to live in our apartment if we both worked for the pachinko parlor. We'd find ourselves out on the streets and out of a job. And we had no other home to go to.

When I got back to work, Hara asked me how it had gone. He seemed pretty worried. I explained the situation and he went to search for a low-cost clinic. He came back with a piece of paper with a name, address, and telephone number, and a map of how to get there.

I went right away. The clinic was in an old office building. For a medical facility it seemed kind of unsanitary, and the equipment was all very basic. There was only one doctor and one nurse. When the elderly doctor had finished his examination, he said, "You're in danger of having a miscarriage, but with complete bed rest there might be a chance of saving the baby." The kindness in his voice brought tears to my eyes.

"Doctor, I'm afraid I'm not in a position to have a baby right now."

"I see," he answered, and he produced a form from his desk drawer. "Fill this in, put your seal on it, and bring it back to me tomorrow afternoon at two. I'm going to use anesthetic, so don't have anything to eat after nine o'clock tonight. Don't drink anything either."

I went back to work clutching the thin manila envelope containing the permission form. I would have had this baby if I could. Taka and I were married, and I wanted to have a baby with him. If only I could have taken bed rest... I asked Hara for the day off and he gave me two, telling me to make sure I took it easy.

The next day, we took the Tiffany ring that Taka had put on my finger the day he proposed, and pawned it to get the money for the operation. We arrived at the clinic at two o'clock, but stopped in front of the door. It wasn't too late to turn and walk away... I looked at the cracked wall with its peeling paint. It had come to this.

I reached for the rickety doorknob that was covered in green rust, and went into the waiting room. The nurse took the manila envelope from me and handed it to the doctor. As soon as he'd checked the form, he started the operation. He gave me the anesthetic and told me to count to ten after him. But I had always been very difficult to put to sleep and very easy to wake up. I got up to ten but I was still wide awake. The doctor was amazed.

"I don't believe it," he said in a shaky voice. "Takamitsu-san, are you still conscious? Are you a heavy drinker by any chance?"

"No." As I answered, I began to fade...

As I slowly regained consciousness, I opened one heavy eyelid and suddenly felt a crippling pain. I couldn't help crying out.

"Don't move! I'm not done yet." I nodded and tried not to moan with pain.

"Doctor, is Shoko OK? Doctor!" On the other side of the thin wooden door, I could hear Taka's panicked voice. A moment later, I heard the sound of something metallic being put down by my head.

"That's it. All finished." At the sound of those words, I felt the strength drain out of my body. The doctor sounded relieved as he told me, "I've been a doctor for forty years and I've never met anyone so resistant to anesthetic. You were really brave. Anyway, you'll be fine now. I may be getting old, but I haven't lost any of my skill."

He moved me from the operating table to the bed. The room didn't seem to get much sunlight, and there was green mold on the pillow. Far worse than the pain of the operation was the regret I felt for the child I'd lost. The tears poured down my face onto the pillow. Taka came in and sat by the bed.

"It was the right decision," he said. "There was nothing else we could do. Don't beat yourself up about it." He took my hand and pressed it to his cheek, but he couldn't look me in the eye. Reality was harsh for us right then.

There was no time for my body or my heart to heal before I had to go back to work. We both worked our butts off, and finally our first month's paychecks arrived. On our day off, we went to a department store in Yokohama and bought the local specialty—Bay Bridge sable cookies— and sent them to Mom back in Osaka with a letter I'd written.

Dear Mom,

I know I haven't always been the best daughter in the past. I'm sure I gave you many sleepless nights. You know, I did feel guilty about all the stuff I did, but I guess I was too selfish to stop going out and having a good time. I'm sorry I'm writing all this in a letter, but I just haven't been able to find a way to say it to your face. Now I'm going to start doing the right thing for once. Taka and I are going to work really hard and make you proud. I love you, Mom. Look after yourself, and please try to take it easy.

Shoko.

I heard from Dad that when Mom read my letter she held it to her heart and, with a smile like the sun breaking through on a cloudy day, said, "We don't have to worry about Shoko-chan anymore."

She suffered a stroke two days later.

Dad called us at work to tell us the bad news. When we told Hara, he urged us to go to see her right away. He took ¥100,000 out of his own wallet.

"You're short of cash, right? Take this."

"We can't give it all back right away. Can we pay you back in installments?"

"What are you talking about? It's an emergency. Pay it back anytime. I can't let you have more than a couple of days, Takamitsu, but Shoko, go ahead and take as long as you need. I'll talk to the owner myself. Look, forget about the rest of today. You should get yourselves to Osaka as fast as you can."

"Thank you. We'll call when we get there," we told him, bowing gratefully. We ran home to quickly pack our bags and then took the next bullet train for Osaka. We arrived at the hospital to find Mom in intensive care. With only a machine to keep her heart beating, she looked like a robot. Little tubes coiled around her body like a spider's web. She didn't look like my mom anymore.

I grabbed the doctor's shoulder. "Will an operation cure her? Is there something you can do for her? We'll pay anything it takes, but please help my mother. I'm begging you."

"A vein has ruptured in the rear part of her brain that can't be operated on. I'm afraid there's nothing we can do. We can only wait for her heart to stop," he answered matter-of-factly.

There was a whirring sound like an insect's wings somewhere in the back of my head and everything went black. When I woke up, I was lying on a hospital bed.

"Shoko, are you OK?"

Taka had been sitting on a sofa over by the wall, waiting for me to come round.

"How's Mom?" I asked, sitting up.

"They moved her to a private room." When I heard this, I got off the bed and stuck my feet into a pair of hospital slippers.

"What room is she in?"

"Are you feeling well enough to walk around?"

"Yeah. It's nothing—just anemia. I'm fine."

"OK... In here." Taka took my hand and led me to my mother's room.

As soon as I saw her face, I slumped to the floor in floods of tears. "Oh Mom! Why did this have to happen?"

Taka stood over me with a sympathetic expression on his face. He knew how deeply I cared about my mother. When I'd been writing that letter to her, he'd asked me what I'd put in it.

"I'm too embarrassed to show you," I'd answered.

"You don't need to show me, but tell me what you said."

"I told her I was sorry for everything I've done."

"Do you want to go shopping tomorrow and get something to send her?"

"Good idea. A present from my first paycheck."

"She'll like that. I'll help you choose something."

The next day, as I walked around the candy counter, having a hard time deciding, it was Taka who pointed to the Bay Bridge cookies and said, "How about these? I'm sure she'd love them."

Taka was usually pretty impatient, but at times like these, he always showed his caring side. I wished he could stay with me here in Osaka longer than two days.

I talked on the phone with my brother and sisters to make arrangements. Dad and Daiki both had to work, so they would stop by in the evenings to see how Mom was doing. Maki, Na-chan, and I would take turns so that at least one of us would be with her all the time. That first day, Taka stayed with me too. The next afternoon, when Maki and Na-chan arrived, we swapped with them and went home to take a bath. I made dinner, set it on the table, and sat down opposite Taka. As he was about to start eating, he stopped and looked at me.

"You'd better eat something."

"I'm not hungry."

"You haven't eaten anything since yesterday."

"No, come to think of it, I don't think I have..."

My hand held the chopsticks and physically transported the food to my mouth, but I finished the meal without tasting a thing. The sound of chopsticks scraping on the bowls echoed in the empty kitchen. I squeezed detergent into the sponge, made it foam up, and washed the dishes in silence. It was summer, but the water that came out of the faucet felt icy.

The afternoon of the following day, we took a taxi back to the hospital. Taka seemed worried as he left me alone to look after Mom.

"Shoko, you've got to be strong," he said, squeezing my shoulder. He took a long look at Mom's face before he set off back to Yokohama.

It was almost a week after her stroke that Mom's sweet smell disappeared, and the room began to fill with a foul odor. The smell got stronger every day, and when I tried to bring my face close up to hers, the stench got in my nostrils and I had to turn my head away. Mom wasn't the only brain-dead patient in the world. I wondered if other patients' families had to endure this kind of smell while they watched over their relatives, or was it just us? This suspicion had started to bug me, when one day three young nurses—two female and one male—came in on their morning rounds. Right by my mother's bed, they began a conversation.

"Hey, do you two want to go to karaoke tonight?" asked the male nurse.

"Not if we have to listen to you singing again!"

"Ugh, tell me about it! But I guess if he's paying..." The two women giggled.

"You know, I don't have to take this shit from you two," laughed the guy. "I'm paying, so are you coming or not?"

"OK, OK. We'll go," grinned the first nurse as she peered down at Mom's electrocardiogram.

"No change, right?" The other two double-checked it and the three began to make their way out of the room. That was when I completely lost it.

"Hold it a minute! How dare the three of you treat my mother like that? She's not a fucking corpse!"

"Oh...no, we didn't mean to..." The three of them shook their heads and waved their hands in denial.

"Oh really? You didn't mean to? Go on, try saying that again," I threatened them, raising my right hand.

"Hey, Shoko, stop it! What do you think you're doing?" Dad was suddenly behind me, grabbing my wrist.

"Let go of me!"

"Where do you think you are?" he shouted. I thought how sad Mom would be if I got into a fight here in her room. "Go back over there and calm down!" he ordered, letting go of my wrist.

"And you losers! Are you just going to stand around staring? Get out!" I slammed my fist into the wall and kicked the door as hard as I could.

"Excuse her, she's too hot-blooded. Perhaps if she donated some of that blood it'd cool her off a bit," said Dad, with his typical dry humor.

"No, we're fine. Please excuse us," they said nervously, all bowing in unison. They hurried out of the room.

"Shoko, what's up with you?" Dad lowered himself into a chair next to the bed.

"You know they were going on about karaoke or something right next to Mom."

"Yeah, that's pretty insensitive."

"Well, that's why I got so mad!"

"I understand how you feel, but remember where you are! Why do you let people like that get to you?"

"You're right," I mumbled, looking down. There was blood on my right hand.

"Shoko, I don't have to work today, so why don't you go back to the house?" As he spoke, Dad was holding onto the rail on the side of Mom's bed looking at her face.

"No, I'm going to stay here tonight."

"I'll stay too."

"Dad, you should go home."

I said this because there was only one sofa in the room. If two people stayed the night, one person would have to sleep on the sofa cushions spread on the hard floor, and the other on the cushionless sofa. Whichever way, it would be hard on Dad, so once it got dark I persuaded him to go home for the night.

A few days later, when Mom was having her diaper changed, I noticed her groin area was bright red from bedsores.

"Excuse me, do you have any ointment you could put on that?" I said to the nurse.

"Ointment? She doesn't need it. Tendo-san is brain-dead, so she can't feel any pain or itching."

"That's true, but if this was your relative would you be able to put up with such lousy treatment?"

"Well, I…" Her voice trailed away.

"You all work in the brain surgery ward, so I guess this is just a job to you. But you know, even if she'll never have a normal life again, my mom is officially alive until her heart stops beating. If you don't understand that, then you shouldn't be working as a nurse!"

The nurse hurriedly put ointment on Mom. "I'm sorry," she said, bowing her head, and left the room. There was something horribly callous about this half-hearted attitude.

I tried to remember the last time I had been so angry. In my yanki days, I would pick fights over dumb stuff like gang pride or just to look cool. I'd had "angry" down to an art form back in those wild days. I remembered how one time I was talking to a friend on the phone and Dad told me off for swearing. When I talked back to him, he snatched the receiver and hit me over the head with it. Mom was always saying "Shoko-chan, can't you try to be more ladylike?" She said it so often it became a catchphrase. Now I'd finally grown up enough to understand how my attitude had bothered my parents, but it was too late. I sat down by the bed and looked at Mom's face.

"Mom, I'm so sorry."

After a while, another nurse came in.

"It smells bad in here, doesn't it? Let's rinse out her mouth."

She took a syringe, filled it with water, and sprayed it into Mom's mouth. As if by magic, the bad smell in the room was gone.

"Why didn't anyone do this before? I had no idea you could do that! What kind of excuse for a hospital is this?"

"Well, I don't really know about the other nurses here…"

There was no point in taking my anger out on her. She wasn't like the other insensitive nurses. She'd noticed the smell immediately and done something about it right away. Did the other nurses not know how to do this simple task? Or did they know but they couldn't be bothered? Or did they not even notice the smell because they didn't care? I was utterly sick of their bad attitude.

The sweltering heat of the summer continued day in, day out, along with the constant buzz of the cicadas. But suddenly one evening, the cicadas fell quiet, and Mom's hospital room felt somehow different. Now, all I could hear was the regular beeping of the ECG, which reminded me of a digital alarm clock going off continuously, and the scuba-diver sound of the artificial respirator. These noises began to irritate me, so I turned on the portable CD player that someone had brought in, and played some music with the volume turned down low.

The day was ending, and the sky was turning pink. I lowered my gaze from the sky to the trees and caught sight of the cast-off skin of a cicada falling to the ground. I'd heard somewhere that cicadas only had a lifespan of a few weeks. Their precious short life was spent braving the heat of summer, single-mindedly calling out for a mate, then, when they finally stopped singing, they slipped from the tree that had been their home and returned to the ground. They leave behind the only home they've ever known and die. By now, the house I'd grown up in had been demolished, and there was no trace of it left. And I was about to experience the pain of loss once again…

I lost track of time as I sat there thinking. Stars began to appear as tiny pinpoints of light in the evening sky. Suddenly a strong gust of wind shook the green leaves. It was as if Mom was trying to say her last good-bye. I took her hand in mine.

"Please don't die, Mom. I was going to be a really good daughter to you. Please don't leave me. I don't want to be alone."

I couldn't stop crying. Then I noticed one single tear was rolling down her cheek.

"Mom!"

She couldn't speak, but she had managed to communicate with me. I felt that she was telling me she loved me. I gently brushed the tear from her cheek and looked at her warm, kind face. Mom. Wherever I'd been, whatever I'd been doing, she had been there for me. I wished I could have heard her comforting voice say, "Shoko-chan, you're home!" just one more time. The music had stopped, and now it was the sound of my sobbing that drowned out the sound of the respirator.

The next day, August 28, 1991, at 8:03 a.m., my mother passed away, at the age of fifty-nine. She left this world as suddenly as that gust of wind through the leaves. As we accompanied my mother's body out of the hospital, the hospital director and nurses lined up and joined their hands in prayer. These people had been totally insensitive the whole time, and now in front of the hospital director they were pretending to have tears in their eyes. What acting talent! I was sure the director couldn't imagine how negligent the treatment and arrogant the attitude they showed to his patients. I guess human beings have the ability to shed tears for their own benefit, even when they're not suffering, even when they're not sad.

The coffin was loaded into the hearse, and we headed for the funeral home. There were white chrysanthemums on the altar. Mom's face smiled down at us from an old snapshot that had been blown up and placed in a frame with a black ribbon.

"This room is for the female family members to get changed." An attendant indicated a door.

I hadn't worn a kimono since the *shichigosan* children's festival when I was seven. I had smiled proudly for the photographer, while Dad stood behind with a hand on my shoulder. Mom held one of my hands and I had a bag of candies in the other. It all seemed a very long time ago.

I went into the changing room, where Mom's sisters and other relatives were being dressed in black kimonos in front of a large full-length mirror. I went up to one of the attendants and spoke to her privately.

"Would it be possible for me to change separately?"

The attendant looked surprised.

"I'm sorry, but we only have one room for women."

"In that case, I'll change later," I said, uncomfortably.

"There's only one specialist to help with the kimonos, so it'd be better if you changed together."

"I don't want anyone to see my tattoo."

"What? Oh, I see." She went over to the specialist dresser and whispered something to her behind her hand.

When I'd first come to Yokohama, Maki had seen my tattoo. She got really mad.

"What were you thinking? You're a woman, for God's sake! If Mom and Dad found out, it'd break their hearts. You'll regret it one day."

"I'll never regret it."

"Yeah, right! What a dumb-ass thing to do!"

She had turned away angrily.

And now she whispered to me gloatingly, "I told you it'd cause problems!" Still, she did manage to get all the other relatives out of the room so I could get changed.

I was the last to arrive in the funeral hall. We all gathered for a family photo in front of the altar.

"Poor Shoko, that high collar looks so uncomfortable," said Maki, in a sarcastic voice. She couldn't drop the subject of my tattoo.

"Maki-chan, did you bring any of Mom's makeup?"

"Yeah, right here."

I took out Mom's lipstick and brush. When I opened her powder compact, it gave off her familiar perfume. Somehow, over time, Mom's perfectly made up face had been replaced by that of a deeply wrinkled old woman. I decided I wanted to send her to heaven looking beautiful. I began to apply her lipstick, but my hand was shaking so much it took me more than half an hour to finish her whole face.

Each funeral guest took a single flower and placed it in Mom's coffin, said their good-byes to her, then she was taken from the funeral home to the crematorium. I watched the furnace door close on her coffin. When we left the building, I looked up and watched the white smoke billowing into the sky. Mom was heading straight for heaven. When the fire went out, the undertaker opened up the door of the furnace, collected the ashes and bones, and placed them on a table.

"Excuse me, was she your mother?" he asked me, removing his gloves.

"Yes, she was."

"How old was she when she passed away?"

"Fifty-nine."

"She was still young. I'm truly sorry."

Mom's brittle bones looked like coral with their thousands of tiny holes. It had taken forever to pick them all up. The undertaker must have seen how advanced her osteoporosis was and started to worry they'd got her age wrong on the memorial tablet.

Right before she had the stroke, she had eaten a light meal with my dad.

"That was delicious, but I'm feeling a little tired now," she'd said when they'd finished. "I think I'll go and lie down."

"Are you all right?" Dad had asked her.

"Oh, I'm fine. Thanks."

She had never opened her eyes again. Her mind set on buying a little house for us all to live in together, she'd worked as hard as she possibly could to make that dream reality, but in the end she was too weak and had just got too tired. So she'd thanked her precious husband, with whom she'd been through all the good and bad times, and left this world.

I kept thinking about the time I'd been sick, woken up to find Mom gone, and run barefoot down the street looking for her. Now, no matter how much I searched for her, she wouldn't be there. My tears wouldn't stop falling.

CHAPTER EIGHT

Chains

After Mom died, Dad gave up the house they'd been renting together. Na-chan went to live with my brother so she could finish high school. Dad decided that there was more work for him up in Yokohama than the Osaka area, and he moved in with Maki.

One day, about six months after that, Hara came up to us looking worried. He'd had a dispute with the owner of the pachinko parlor over management policies.

"If I could stand it here, I'd stay and look after you two. The money's OK, but I just can't take it anymore. I'm quitting at the end of the month," he told us. "If you come with me, I'll make sure there's work for you. You might have a hard time of it, but it could work out for you. What do you think?"

By now, Taka and I loved Hara like a brother, so we didn't even have to think about it. We quit the pachinko parlor, took the little savings we had, and moved into a one-room apartment in Tokyo. Hara got Taka a job in a consumer loan company, and I took a job in a bar in Shinjuku working ten-hour shifts from seven in the evening until five in the morning. But after a short time, it turned out Hara had to leave Tokyo and return to his hometown in Kumamoto in southern Japan.

"Don't forget all the things I taught you. I hope you'll have your own loan company someday," he said, smiling, as we saw him off at the airport.

Now our closest friend was gone, and we realized we had no one here in Tokyo to depend on, and no home elsewhere to go back to.

My decision to work as hard as I could to help look after my family meant that I was always putting too much pressure on myself. One problem was all the money I had to lend Maki because of Itchan's gambling. He couldn't stick with a job, and instead scrounged money off his own parents to live. Maki's life was miserable. She couldn't go out to work because of the baby, and was heavily in debt to a bunch of loan sharks. Before long, she began to turn to me for money.

Soon I was handing her money right and left every month. But even this wasn't enough, and she started borrowing from Dad as well. Then Dad started to feel the pinch, and he in turn came to borrow from me. I felt like a dog chasing its tail—the harder I worked, the faster my money slipped away, and I could never catch up with it. And gradually, as Itchan and Maki's debts ballooned, even Taka got involved.

I had thought that coming to terms with Mom's death would get easier as time went on, but instead the pain of missing her only grew stronger. It got to the stage where it was the only thing I could think about. At the time of her death, I'd weighed a hundred and five pounds, but now I'd dropped to ninety-five. Luckily, I got a raise, and for the sake of my health I asked to have my working hours cut to a four-hour shift from eight till midnight.

One Sunday, Taka suggested we go out to eat, so we headed for a *shabu shabu* restaurant. A large copper pot of boiling water sat in the middle of the table next to a mountain of vegetables and a plate of beef. The stacks of thinly sliced meat made me think of the decks of playing cards at the casinos my clients took me to. I remembered when we'd gone out for a meal as a family when I was a kid, Mom would laugh and say,

"Food always tastes better when we eat together like this."

"What's wrong?" Taka used his beer mug to push the little bowl of sesame dipping sauce out of the way, and set his beer down.

"I wish Mom could have been here."

"Shoko, your mom isn't with us anymore. How long are you going to keep this up?"

"I know, but..."

"I'm still here."

The steam from the cooking pot obscured Taka's face, and although he was right across the table, he looked miles away to me.

I guess it was around that time that I started to become emotionally unstable. I got upset over trivial things, and outside work I barely spoke a word to anyone. I started seeing a doctor, who diagnosed severe depression and put me on medication.

It was the beginning of the 1990s, and the booming prosperity that Japan had enjoyed in the 1980s was over. The economic bubble had burst, and business at the bar was really slow. In the past, it had been easy to meet the monthly cash quotas that each hostess had to bring in, but now clients just weren't spending like they used to. Still, I kept handing over money to Maki, regular as clockwork. I didn't want to get Taka sucked any further into the mess of my family affairs, so every day I struggled to get myself to work. But the more I tried to solve the situation by myself, the worse my mental state became.

I turned twenty-four, but things still weren't looking up for me. My life was full of the same old problems, and I was getting sick and tired of everything. I kept trying to persuade Maki to divorce Itchan, but she wouldn't listen. She always stuck up for him, reminding me how they had a child to look after, telling me what a good man he was really, and how he was going to get back on the straight and narrow any time now. It was the same way I'd felt about Ito. No matter how much he punched or kicked me, I forgave him because I was in love with him. Maki had lived far away from me during my relationship with Ito, but she'd been worried sick. She used to be in tears when she called me on the phone to beg me to hurry up and end it with him. "He's married and all he does is hit you. How can he really love you? Haven't you had enough of being someone's mistress?" she used to ask. Now I realized everything she had said was right on the mark. Was Maki going to have to go through the same kind of hell herself before she came to her senses?

My weight was down to eighty-eight pounds, and I was so pale I must have looked like some kind of emaciated ghost. But I was so depressed and deluded that when I looked in the mirror I thought I looked fine.

I had nightmares every night. Flashbacks of the bad old days, pretending to enjoy the cakes and stuff Dad brought home, all the while watching to make sure he wasn't going to go into one of his rages... The old hell of my schooldays when I was bullied for being fat...

Blimp! Pig!

I used to wake up panting and soaked in sweat, with the old taunts ringing in my ears.

I can't go back to that again. I can't get fat!

I would grab my bottle of tranquilizers from the drawer and swallow down a handful. I knew I couldn't continue being so obsessed with my body, yet I couldn't bring myself to eat anything. Eventually, I realized I had a serious eating disorder. And still Maki would come to me in tears asking for cash.

One night I dreamed that the dragon from Maejima's tattooed back was winding itself snakelike around my body. My mind replayed snatches of conversation from the past.

Shoko, get your ass over here.

Get off me!

Your father has nowhere else to squeeze a penny from.

Yeah, I guess...

If it wasn't for me he'd be finished.

"No!" I screamed at the top of my lungs and opened my eyes. The sweat was running from my temples down the back of my neck, and my heart was hammering in my chest. No matter how much I struggled, money was a chain that bound me.

Ever since my mother died, I hadn't had any kind of sexual relationship with Taka. I would have liked to go back to the way things used to be between us, but both my body and mind were in too bad a shape. Sometimes it felt as though I was running through a pitch black tunnel but could never get the end in sight. I hated myself for being so weak. Even so, I didn't skip a day of work.

Twenty-five years old and eighty-six pounds. My weight was leaving me as fast as the money I was doling out to Maki. I wished I could talk to Mom. No matter how much I worked, it wasn't enough. I was such a burden to Taka. All these thoughts made me dizzy. If I managed to put anything into my mouth and swallow, I would immediately feel nauseous and have to throw it all up again. When the two of us had moved from Yokohama to Tokyo we'd been dirt poor, but at least we'd been happy. On our days off, we'd gone out to visit the department stores and even though we couldn't afford to buy anything, we'd been satisfied with a ¥300 glass of freshly pressed orange juice at the concession stand in the station. For lunch, we'd eat soba noodles at a stand-up counter, ordering two bowls of the cheapest on the menu, and sharing one potato and meat croquette.

"Here's hoping next time we'll be able to have one each," I'd laugh as I cut the croquette in half with my chopsticks.

At night, we'd laugh and joke all the way along the narrow, unlit street to the convenience store, and the long walk would seem short. We'd buy one can of beer and one soda, one sweet snack and one salty, and enjoy them after dinner. How could I be the same person who used to take such delight in eating? What had I turned into? I was sucked into a whirlpool of self-loathing.

One day I got a call from Dad.

"Maki needs money. Is there anything you can do?"

"What? I loaned her ¥70,000 just yesterday morning! Then in the evening she came to me crying that Itchan had stolen it from her and she couldn't pay off her bills, so I gave her another ¥70,000 before I went out to work. I gave away ¥140,000 in a single day. I can't afford to do that again today."

"I know it's bad asking you to help all the time, but she has nowhere else to turn. You've got to help her. She's your sister."

"OK...," I said, inwardly sighing.

"I'm sorry, but I need to ask a favor of Takamitsu too. Could you get him to transfer ¥100,000 to my account? I promise I'll pay it back."

"Dad, why—" I began, then stopped and checked myself. "Yeah, sure. Taka'll be glad to help you out."

How had the father I'd been so afraid of become this meek little man begging on Maki's behalf? Even when she'd been a yanki, Maki had been a total daddy's girl and confessed to him everything she did. Dad, too, had talked about all kinds of things with Maki. I guess it was the equivalent of my relationship with Mom.

I talked to Taka, and he transferred the ¥100,000 to Dad's bank account. It didn't make any difference that the name on the account wasn't hers, it was obvious the money was going straight to Maki. How much money were those people getting through?

I'd had a fever for about a week and it wasn't getting any better, so Taka took me to the hospital. They ran some tests and found that I had a kidney problem. The doctor told me I needed dialysis and handed me a form to fill out and sign before my next visit. I sat there shell shocked, but as usual Taka was there for me. He promised me he'd do anything it took to get me better. But the cost of dialysis was way too high for us. And it was something I'd have to do for the rest of my life. Could I possibly be any more of a burden to Taka? The next day I saw Taka off to work as usual, locked the door behind him, and went back into the apartment. I just wanted to sleep, to see nothing, to hear nothing.

I'd been trying my best not to take the sleeping pills that the doctor kept giving me. Now I took the bottles of pills that had been piling up in the sideboard drawer, tipped about a hundred pills into my mouth, a few at a time, and washed them down with water. I sat on the floor with my back against the refrigerator and watched the world turn red and black before my eyes. As I faded out of consciousness, I saw an image of my blood backtracking into a syringe. Present and past had come together... I felt as if I had pulled off the chains that had been choking me and at last I could relax. I couldn't see or hear anything anymore...

Taka got home from work to find me collapsed in front of the refrigerator and called an ambulance, but I was already close to death. While I was in the ambulance, my heart stopped, but they managed to resuscitate me. It stopped again in the hospital elevator. Again, they got me back and wheeled me into surgery. There my heart stopped for the third time, and the doctor came to inform Taka.

"You'd better contact her other family members. We'll do everything we can, but I think you'd better prepare yourself for the worst."

"What?"

"Your wife is in critical condition. Even if we manage to save her, there's a strong chance she'll be in a persistent vegetative state. It's likely that she sustained permanent brain damage when her heart stopped."

Leaving Taka with this devastating news, he closed the operating room door. After a while, the red light that indicated an operation was in progress went off.

I was in a coma for a week. I remember feeling as if I was in a wide-open, empty black space. I was hurrying ahead, but I could vaguely hear someone way behind me calling my name.

I have to hurry.

I took a big step forward and just as my foot touched the ground, I heard, "Shoko!"

I realized I'd heard Dad's voice, and in that moment I became aware of a bright white light shining into my eyes. There by my hospital bed stood Dad, Taka, and Maki.

"Shoko! I can't bear to lose anybody else!" Dad said, squeezing my hand. He was crying, something he hadn't even done when Mom had died.

"I'm sorry," I whispered through my oxygen mask. That was the most painful thing—not what I'd been through myself, but the fact that I had made others cry over me. Seeing Dad cry for the first time in my life was a huge jolt of reality. This time I was going to get back on my feet.

A month later, I was so happy to get out of the hospital and be back home. It was only a tiny one-room apartment, but to me it was the best place in the world. Luckily, I'd escaped any brain damage. My kidney problem had been weighing on my mind, but I had it checked out in more detail, and they decided I didn't need dialysis after all. Unfortunately, because of the tube they'd put down my throat in the hospital, I couldn't get any water down and I had to suck on pieces of ice. Of course, I couldn't eat any kind of food at all either, and my weight dropped even further to eighty-four pounds.

Taka kept bugging me. "You need to put on some weight. You know, women are cute when they're a little chubby."

And finally, after all that had happened, I learned to see things as they were, rather than through my warped mind.

"Well," said the doctor, when I asked him if putting on weight would make me get better, "your bodily functions are rather weak, so it may take time to reach a healthy weight again. I advise you to try and be patient."

I spent my days at home with a new positive outlook, trying to get myself back to normal. I began to eat properly, but my body had taken so much punishment that I had to struggle to get my weight up to the ninety-pound mark. But I kept trying, and after another six months, I was much healthier.

I'd always been interested in cosmetics, and I made up my mind to put my hobby to practical use by enrolling at a professional makeup school. To tell the truth, I wanted to learn how to hide my facial scars. They weren't that obvious, but it wasn't unusual for people to look closely and ask me what had happened to my face, or if I'd been in an accident. This wasn't the only legacy of the beatings of the past. Although I tried not to let it bother me, on the day before rain was due, or other times when the humidity in the air was high, the various parts of my body that had been injured would start to ache. And Taka and I were still not having sex. We'd even stopped talking about the subject. I began to be afraid of losing my identity as a woman. I'd stand in front of the mirror staring at my own reflection, and all I could see were those scars.

I did really well at makeup school, and every time I left the house I'd spend almost two hours beforehand carefully following all the steps I'd learned, but I couldn't successfully hide my own scars. I'd never been confident about my looks, but now these scars had given me an even worse complex. I thought it over a long time before eventually going to see a plastic surgeon. He told me he couldn't get rid of the scars completely, but he could fix it so they'd be invisible with makeup. It wasn't the answer I'd been hoping for. Still, a few days after my twenty-seventh birthday I found the courage to have the operation. As the doctor had promised, my scars became easy to hide. It may not have been much, but I did feel better. And then an amazing thing happened. One day when I was all dressed up and out shopping in Shinjuku, I was scouted by some guys on the street who were hiring hostesses. It was about time I started working again, so I let them show me around their fancy Shinjuku club. The pay was good, so I decided to take the job.

I began working, and suddenly I had a whole new life that revolved around my job. I got up mid-morning, watched the news on TV, and read the newspaper from cover to cover, including local and international news, and even the financial and political sections, which had never held any interest for me before. I was determined to be able to hold conversations with all sorts of clients. I'd eat a late breakfast, and then clients would start to call me. If they were asking me to meet them before work and then accompany them to the club, I'd leave the house earlier than usual, get my hair done, and go to meet them for dinner. If I was going to do this job at all, then I was going to give it my best shot. I planned to become more than just one of the nameless extras who helped out the top hostesses. I wanted to be the club's number one earner.

Sometimes it felt like I'd gone back in time when I was with some of my clients. They were like relics of the bubble era the way they threw their money around. And in this flamboyant universe, there was a lot of fierce competition between the hostesses. Work didn't end when the club closed. We would usually go on somewhere else for drinks with valued clients, and I never got home before the small hours.

One night after getting home late as usual, I whispered in Taka's ear, "Do you wanna have sex?"

"Huh?"

"Come on Taka, make love to me."

"What are you talking about? You know your body's not a hundred percent yet. You don't have to do this."

"No, I want to."

"Aren't you tired? It's late."

"Not really."

"I'm good, OK? Go to sleep."

"Oh . . ." It felt like a slap in the face. There was nothing left to say but good night.

As I lay on the bed staring at Taka's back, I was reminded of lying in bed all alone when I was little, longing to curl up with Mom and feel the warmth of her body next to mine. That night I hardly slept.

I was pretty much preoccupied with work and handing out cash as usual to Maki, but whenever I thought of all the problems my family was causing for Taka, I felt terrible. He was working all hours of the day and night to help them out, and he never complained. We seemed to be at home at completely different times and barely saw each other anymore. I would make a pot of rice and leave him something in the refrigerator to heat up in the microwave. I wished I could be at home more often, but it was impossible. My work required me to be available twenty-four hours. I had to be constantly on my guard in case some other hostess tried to lure my clients away from me, and I had to be very picky about who to take on as clients in the first place. The best way to escape all the bitching and competition was to become a top performer.

I thought it all over for several days and came to the conclusion I had to get divorced. Taka had been like a brother in arms to me, helping me through all my troubles. I didn't want to lose him, but I could see no other way out.

"Look, I don't want to cause you any more grief. I think we should split up."

"Don't treat me like I'm some stranger. We're in this together," Taka answered fiercely.

But I had it in my head that as long as he was tied to me, Taka was always going to suffer. Money had bound me to Maejima in the same way, and it had been the cause of so much pain. I asked him again to agree to a divorce. He told me he needed time to think.

"Until I met you, I didn't treat women with respect," he confessed to me a few days later. "I never really understood how they thought, but you know, somehow I really do understand you."

That was all he said before signing the divorce papers and moving out. When I got home after filing the papers, all Taka's things were gone from the apartment. Even his pillow was gone from the bed.

Make love to me. I'd only ever said these words to him once in the five years we were together. Would it have made a difference if he'd said yes? That first night lying there in his arms, I'd asked him to stay with me forever. We'd kissed and made love again. It had felt as if we were sealing the deal. I knew he respected my feelings, but that hadn't been enough for me. I'd needed to go back to that physical intimacy too.

We'd always told each other that we ought to try to move somewhere bigger, but now, as I looked around our tiny one-room apartment, it felt huge and very empty. Everything in there belonged to me, but my most cherished possession was missing, and I knew I'd never get it back.

On my twenty-ninth birthday, I got home from work to hear the phone ringing. I rushed to pick up.

"Yes?"

"Shoko..."

"Dad, what's the matter?"

"Shoko, I need to you to listen calmly to what I have to say."

I knew something bad was coming.

"OK. What is it?"

"I've got cancer. They say I've got about six months to live."

My mind went blank, and all I could hear for a few moments was a kind of buzzing in my ears. Then my survival reflex kicked in. The noise stopped. "I'm coming over."

"It's late. Don't bother."

"Dad, go back to sleep. I'll be right there."

He had delivered the news of his own death in such a calm, dignified manner, you'd have thought he was talking about someone else.

I put down the phone, rushed out of the apartment, and hailed a cab. I spent the taxi ride thinking over the past. When I was little I had an orange stuffed dog that I'd taken everywhere with me and slept with every night. There was the pocket watch on a silver chain from grandpa, and a decorative wooden comb that Mom had given me as a memento of my grandma. And the pink music box that Mom had picked out for me at the department store. When you opened the lid, you could see a brass cylinder that looked like the stem of a rose, complete with pins that looked like golden thorns, turning slowly around and around. When the pins brushed against the petal-like keys of the tiny keyboard, the tune *Romance* from the movie *Jeux interdits* would play. I loved the music so much that I would wind it up dozens of times a day. Even when the music box stopped working, I used to polish it until it shone and proudly kept it on display on a bookshelf. Then there was the kaleidoscope that Mom had bought me. The first time we looked through it together, we saw a pattern like the glittering fish scales on the back of one of our koi. But no matter how many times I twisted it and held it up to the light after that, it never showed me that same beautiful pattern again. I'd loved these things so much as a kid, but they'd all gone missing over the years. I wondered why I was thinking about these lost things now.

I arrived at Maki's place and was taking off my shoes at the front door, when Dad appeared.

"Thanks for coming," he said, with a big smile.

"Dad, is it really cancer?"

"I'd been getting a lot of stomach pains. I've had a weak stomach since way back, but it was getting pretty bad so I had it checked out, and that's when they found it. I'm not worried about you, but Maki, well…" He paused. "She's up to her neck in debt, she's got the kid to look after, and that husband of hers… Don't know what she's going to do."

Dad looked exactly the same as always. I made him tell me exactly what they'd said at the hospital. "Your routine neglect of your health has had a terrible effect on your body," the doctor had begun, and then proceeded to lecture Dad, who already had mild diabetes. According to Dad, the doctor was still talking as he stuck a camera down his throat to take a look at his stomach, but had suddenly shut up when he saw the tumor. But my dad wasn't one to be put off easily. He'd forced the doctor to admit he'd got cancer. Apparently the tumor looked malignant, and the doctor reckoned he had about six months at the most to live. At which, Dad had announced he was going home. No amount of persuasion on the part of the doctor would make him stay. According to Dad, the conversation had gone something like this:

"Well, I'd better get moving. No time to hang around here. I've got a lot to do."

"Tendo-san, what are you saying? You don't want to be hospitalized?"

"No need."

"How about anticancer drugs?"

"No thanks."

"The pain is going to be unbearable. Please let us admit you."

"No."

I could just imagine him turning and marching out of the doctor's office, a swagger in his step.

"Dad, go to the hospital. Please!" I begged, as soon as he finished his story.

"No. I want to be there for Maki for as long as I can. Shoko, you will take her of her for me, won't you?"

"Dad..." I couldn't believe that even though he had no idea if he was going to live another day, he was fretting over Maki.

And so without taking a single drug, Dad began his fight against cancer. I couldn't help wondering if there was some operation that would prolong his life a little, but I kept it to myself. I buried myself in my job and accepted that Dad was dying. I'd made it to number two at the club, but the number three girl was never far behind.

"Could you lend us some money?"

As Dad lay on his futon fighting the pain, Itchan's parents knelt by him and bowed their heads to the tatami matting. Somehow they'd found out that Dad had been paid ¥800,000 for a job he did just before he got sick. Thanks to Itchan, their spoiled only son, they'd lost the family home along with the land it was built on. They'd gone on the lam and had started renting an apartment nearby.

"I don't know how much you're going to need, so take what you want," answered Dad, handing over his bankbook and personal seal. Itchan's parents went to the bank and took out the whole ¥800,000. I heard the story when I went to visit Dad on my day off. When Itchan came wandering in without a care in the world, despite losing at poker yet again, I grabbed him by the collar and got right in his face.

"What kind of a sleazebag sends his own parents to beg for money from a dying man? I'll fucking kill you!" I fumed, kicking over a chair as I shoved him back out of the front door.

"Hey, cool it. What's your problem?"

"Shoko! Stop it! Dad'll hear. Calm down," said Maki, who had run out to see what was going on.

"Oh, is there something you don't want Dad to hear?" I asked sarcastically.

"I let it slip to my in-laws that Dad had just been paid. Itchan doesn't know anything about it."

"What? My folks scored some dough from your dad?"

"That's right!" My voice was trembling with rage.

Maki tried to intervene by dragging Itchan inside.

"I haven't finished yet!" I followed them in and kicked the door shut.

"Shoko, I'm totally bummed my parents did that."

"You know Itchan, I've never once asked you to pay me back what you've borrowed. And you've never made any effort of your own to pay it back either. You take advantage of everybody's good nature and then trample all over them. Well, you're not getting away with that kind of shit this time. You're going to give back every penny you took from my dad!"

"Sure I will. I promise, OK? Sorry..."

"Shoko, it's all my fault. I'm sorry about Itchan." Maki looked shame-faced. "Really, I'm so sorry."

"I'm going to speak to Dad and then I'm leaving." I went into his room and stood there for a moment until I'd calmed down. Then I knelt next to his futon.

"Dad, are you sure you won't have the operation?"

"No point. It won't cure me. But it might help if you quit yelling like that and try not to argue with your sister."

"Sorry."

"You know, when you were little, you were always the easy one to manage. Even when you were in kindergarten, you'd get up in the morning and get yourself ready. I used to say I'd take you, but you always said you could walk there by yourself. Maki was the one who whined and clung to me. She was always bugging me for this or that. You acted so grown up it was almost frightening. You were so quiet I never knew what you were thinking. When you were arrested, do you know why I never came to see you?"

Every time Maki was arrested, Dad had gone in to pick her up. When she'd been kept at the detention center and then transferred to juvie, he visited her all the time.

"Why?"

"I tried everything, including hitting you, to try to make you get your act together. Maki would cry and tell me she was sorry, but you wouldn't even respond. In the end, you'd just go and do what you wanted all over again. I never had a clue what you were thinking. I wanted to visit you when you were arrested, but I didn't think it would be good for you. You'd never change your attitude if I did. I had to abandon you... I hated doing it to you, but I believed that you'd straighten things out by the end. You took all this from me and still managed to forgive me. And now here you are, so grown up. Back in those days, I couldn't imagine ever being able to talk to you like this. You never know how things are going to turn out." He smiled and stroked my head.

"No matter how much you hit me, you were always my dad."

In my teens I'd felt that Dad had always had his back to me. I wanted him to turn around and see me. Just once would have been enough. When I couldn't get his attention, it had felt as if my heart was breaking with loneliness. I hadn't been afraid of being hit, I'd been afraid that he didn't love me anymore. I guess that's why I'd been remembering things I'd loved as a kid but lost as I'd grown up. I'd felt the same way about Dad.

Shortly after I'd been sent to the reform school, a teacher said to me, "Tendo, I've noticed you do your chores and make sure everything's cleaned up properly even when the teachers aren't watching. And you never get annoyed at the selfish ones who won't do anything. I've never seen a girl like you. I can't understand how someone like you ended up in here."

That was the kind of thing all the adults around me used to say. I was totally mysterious to them. But quite simply, the reason I turned bad wasn't the fault of anyone else, or my environment. I wanted to have fun, and I did. I'd always been weak, but I pretended to be tough, and having friends to hang out with had been an awesome feeling. I had felt totally at home on the city streets at night. I was just a kid who did whatever she wanted.

"I won't be able to get there myself now, but would you try to find Fujisawa-san's grave and thank her for me?"

"Sure, Dad."

The old lady had been so good to him, but ever since he'd got out of the hospital, our family had been in so much turmoil that he hadn't even been able to go and pay his respects. Funnily enough, I'd been thinking about the exact same thing. It was uncanny how Dad and I were so alike. I felt how strong our blood ties really were.

It wasn't long before Dad's health started to deteriorate daily. One day he said to me, "Takamitsu isn't much of a talker, but he's a good man. He's a keeper, that one. He really cares about you, too. Why don't you bring him to see me, there's something I want to say to him. You know, I never managed to be much of a father to you two."

I'd kept the divorce a secret from Dad, but I suspected he already knew about it. The tattoo on his back was of Jibo Kannon, the Buddhist goddess of mercy, whose name means "loving mother." Perhaps she had been watching over me with a mother's love. Maybe that's why Dad could read my mind.

"I'll bring him next week."

"Yes, I'd like that," he answered with a smile, and as we waved good-bye, I noticed how frail his hand had become.

I had every intention of keeping my promise to Dad, so the next week Taka and I arrived at Yokohama Station. We sat in silence in the cab all the way to Maki's apartment. When we arrived, there was an ambulance parked outside with its back doors open.

Please don't let it be Dad.

But two paramedics came out of the building with Dad on a stretcher, and Maki close behind, bawling her eyes out. I leapt out of the taxi and ran up to them.

"Dad! It's Shoko. Can you hear me?" I shouted.

"Shoko, please forgive Maki. Do it for me," he whispered in a feeble voice, then he closed his eyes and seemed to fall asleep.

At the hospital, he was taken straight to intensive care. The doctor blocked our way as we tried to follow. "Please wait outside. He's too weak to speak to you right now." He closed the door on us.

Through the small window in the door, we could see people rushing around. Maki was sitting in the smoking area, crying, "Daddy! Daddy!" Her legs were shaking uncontrollably.

"Shoko, I've caused Dad nothing but worry," she sobbed.

"Maki-chan," I sighed, and let my head slide down the wall until I was slumped on the floor.

The door opened and a nurse appeared. "Please come inside quickly!" she called. But as we got to the door, we heard the long, extended *peeeep* of the ECG and saw the line go flat. The doctor looked at his watch.

"Time of death, 10:12 a.m."

He died on October 5, 1997. At the age of seventy, Dad, along with his tattoo of Jibo Kannon, joined Mom in heaven.

Maki fell to her knees and began to bawl at the top of her voice. I sat there letting my tears stream down, making no attempt to wipe them away.

Dad's body was taken to the funeral home. He looked nothing like he had in those early years when I was scared of him. His face was gentle and serene. Maki went home to fetch a photo and her mourning kimono.

"Dad..." I took his face in my hands and accidentally knocked the cotton wadding out of his right ear. Still-warm blood trickled out onto my hand.

I remembered walking home along a moonlit street after we'd been to some street fair. The goldfish swimming around in its clear plastic bag, a candy apple that gleamed like a piece of ceramic, cotton candy that looked like fluffy snow—I was struggling to carry home a heap of goodies when the loop of string around my little finger slipped off. I cried out and reached on my tiptoes to try to catch the red, rabbit-shaped balloon, but it floated off into the night sky, bobbing as if waving good-bye. Where did that red rabbit balloon get to, I wonder?

I changed into my funeral kimono and began to ring the bell next to the coffin, hoping to help Dad find his way to heaven. The sound echoed in the silent room and reminded me of the sound of the little bell on the talisman that Dad had bought for me that long ago New Year's.

"I'll do it for a while." Maki knelt down next to me on a floor cushion and began to ring the bell.

"Do you want something to eat?" Daiki put a convenience store bag of *onigiri* rice balls on the corner of the altar.

"Shoko..." Na-chan buried her face in my lap.

When I bit into an onigiri, it tasted of salty tears.

Itchan and his parents turned up at the funeral. They bowed and offered their condolences in the correct, formal language. They were about to light some incense when suddenly I couldn't take it anymore. I got to my feet.

"What the hell are you doing here?"

"Shoko, stop it!" said Maki.

"Shut up, Maki!"

"Shoko, please don't get mad." Na-chan came over and tried to hold me back.

"Oh, Na-chan…" I stroked Na-chan's back, my hand trembling. Just then, Taka came back from buying writing paper and envelopes, and he handed them to me along with a ballpoint pen. I wrote a letter to Dad and put it into an envelope with the little talisman and its bell. Then I placed the letter and a single flower in his coffin. I touched his hand for the last time, and it was as hard and cold as ice.

The smoke from Dad's ashes mingled with the autumn rain and disappeared way up into the gray, gloomy sky. I couldn't tell if they were tears or raindrops that poured down my face.

At the crematorium, I watched in disgust as Itchan took the chopsticks and began to pick up Dad's bones.

"Stop! I don't want you to touch him!"

"Shoko, don't you dare talk to my husband like that!" Maki shoved me hard in the shoulder.

"I don't give a shit who he is!"

"Cut it out!" Taka suddenly hollered, and slapped my face for the first time ever.

I went ballistic. "No one tells me what to do! And you three—get out of here!" Mumbling apologies, Itchan and his parents hurriedly bowed and left the building. Daiki, Maki, Na-chan, Taka, and I collected the bones and placed them in a little urn.

Maki took it home with her, warming it with her tears.

CHAPTER NINE

Separate Ways

Dad's death finally brought Maki to her senses, and she filed for divorce. She found herself a hostessing job and came to terms with the fact she was going to be a single mother. She also managed to sort out a monthly plan to pay off all the debts that Itchan had left her. Not surprisingly, Itchan and his parents disappeared with all the money Dad, Taka, and I had loaned them, and we never heard from them again.

I didn't react to Dad's death at all the way I'd reacted to Mom's. It spurred me on to work harder than ever, and I set out to achieve more than I'd ever done before. Even on my days off I would arrange to meet clients for dinner. I hardly ever got in touch with Taka anymore. I devoted all my time to work. There was something very important that I wanted to buy, and so at the age of thirty, for the first time in my life, I opened a savings account.

One day, a letter arrived from Daiki along with a photo. He'd been transferred overseas by his company, and he'd written to tell me that he'd met someone and was planning to get married. In the photo they were both smiling, and her expression reminded me a little of Mom. He sounded incredibly happy. And I couldn't have been happier for him.

I placed the letter in front of Mom and Dad's memorial tablets on the little family altar. I glanced up at their photos and imagined I saw them both smile.

The mama-san of the club where I worked bought me an outfit as a thirty-first birthday present. Of course, she'd noticed that I never wore short sleeves, even in the middle of summer (knowing how sharp she always was, she'd probably guessed about my tattoo), and she'd picked out a long-sleeved suit for me, in shocking pink. It was perfect. As we left the boutique, she smiled and in a mock whisper confided, "You're almost in the number one spot. Just a little more."

I wasn't the only one working this hard—Maki was busting her ass too. For once in her life, she had stopped relying on men, and as a result had discovered her own strengths. She had worked her way up to the top spot at her hostess bar in a very short time. Maki was surprisingly strong-minded, and when the long-timers on the staff made snide comments, it only aroused her fighting instincts. She would grit her teeth and vow to herself that she'd make them eat crow.

I'd ask her if she was looking for a new boyfriend. "It's not that easy to find a good guy these days," she'd shrug. "How about you?"

"I'm too busy with work right now."

"Tell the truth, you still have a thing for Taka, don't you?"

"Stop it!"

"Shoko, I'm sorry. If I'd broken up with Itchan earlier, then I wouldn't have messed things up so badly for you two."

"No, it really wasn't your fault. It was me..."

"Here's to us both finding happiness."

"Right."

"Next time I'm going to catch myself a good one." Maki really looked determined.

"Ha. It's about time."

"Hey, look who's talking. And aren't you the one with the wild tattoo?"

"I thought we agreed not to talk about that."

"I'm sorry, but no matter how old we get, I'm always going to worry about my little sister. We don't have parents to do that for us anymore."

"That's true," I sighed.

"Shoko, do you think you did the right thing with Taka?"

"Yeah, I'm sure."

"Hey, you know what, don't worry about your tattoo. If something like that's a problem to some guy, then he can't be worth it."

"Thanks."

Maki really sounded like my big sister again.

"See you soon," I called as I set off home. Maki stood and waved from her front door until I was out of sight.

I fell asleep to the comfortable rhythm of the train and Hikaru Utada's *Automatic* playing on my Walkman.

By the time I was thirty-two, I had quite a lot of money in the bank. I began to search my neighborhood for a grave plot where Mom and Dad's ashes could be laid to rest, but I couldn't believe how expensive it was. I finally found one on the Internet that looked good, but I had nowhere near enough to buy it. Still, I wasn't going to be put off. Somehow or other, I was going to buy a grave plot, and it was going to be close to my home.

Na-chan called me.

"Shoko, can I come and visit you tomorrow?"

"Sure. What's up?"

"My boyfriend has asked me to marry him, and he says he wants to come and ask permission, but since I don't have parents anymore... Well, I told him he didn't have to be so formal, but he's insisting."

It sounded as if she'd found herself a really nice, polite guy. And when I met him, I wasn't disappointed. Yamamoto was a graphic designer, two years older than Na-chan, decent and reliable. He knelt down in front of Mom and Dad's photos on the altar, joined his hands together, bowed, and in very proper language announced their engagement. A ring sparkled on each of their left hands, and they seemed genuinely happy. After we'd finished dinner, he was considerate enough to realize that Na-chan and I hadn't seen each other in a long while and had a lot to talk about, so he opened up his laptop computer and got some work done while we caught up. Then before we went to bed, he lit some incense and thanked my parents again. I knew there would be no need to worry about Na-chan.

As they were leaving the next morning, Yamamoto turned to me and said, "Thank you for everything. Please come down and stay with us in Hiroshima sometime."

"Thank you. Look after my little sister."

"I will."

"Shoko, take care of yourself. Don't go getting sick, OK?"

I couldn't believe my little sister was worrying about my health. She'd grown up without me noticing. I heaved a sigh of relief.

After they left that morning, I lay down on the sofa. It was one of my rare days off, and I let myself drift into sleep. I was woken by the sound of a car horn in the street below. I ran to the window and looked down. There was a black Infiniti parked outside that I didn't recognize. I was turning to walk away from the window when I heard, "Hey, Shoko!"

"Taka?"

"Come down a minute." I hurried downstairs.

"I know I'm late, but happy birthday." He handed me a bankbook. When I looked inside, there was an account in my name with ¥500,000 in it.

"Put it toward that grave plot," he said.

"How did you know?"

"I know you well enough by now to understand what you're thinking. Give me some credit!"

"But are you sure?"

"This is the only thing I could think of to do for you."

"I heard you have a girlfriend, I—"

He cut me off. "I want to do this for you. I promised your father I'd make you happy, but I never did."

"What are you talking about? You were always good to me."

"And your dad was like a real father to me. Please take it."

"Thanks, Taka."

"Don't work too hard."

"I won't."

"And don't go falling for some scumbag of a guy again, OK?" he said, smiling.

"Yeah, I fall in love so often it's a real danger. But no, I'll never do that again," I answered with a laugh.

"Promise?"

Just as I'd done when he proposed, I looked Taka straight in the eyes and nodded. Taka had never once told me he loved me, but he had always been there for me. Now that he'd made a new life for himself, we couldn't go back. And I had to move forward too. It was time to find my own path in life.

Daiki also put some money into the grave plot fund, and so we were able to buy a plot in the temple where the Edo-era samurai Kagemoto Toyama was buried. Dad had always loved the TV series *Toyama no Kinsan*, which was based on Toyama's life story, so we figured he'd be happy being laid to rest here. If Dad was smiling, then Mom would be at peace by his side.

There was a distinct chill in the air and the days were getting shorter when we finally laid our parents' ashes to rest. When we looked up at the evening sky, the thick cloud of smog that hung over Tokyo glowed a vivid shade of pink. It reminded me of the cherry blossom in our yard, and suddenly I could imagine Mom's smiling face. If I took a deep breath and closed my eyes, I could bring back the good times.

Mom's hand always felt warm when I held it as I walked happily by her side. My wish was that Mom and Dad would be just as comfortable and happy here side by side, and that they would enjoy the cherry blossoms in spring. It was already nine years since Mom's death, and three since Dad's. I thought back over my life and the role my parents had played in it. I lit a candle on their grave, and its flame was blurred by the tears that welled up in my eyes. As it flickered in the wind, it reminded me of those fireflies from the river when I was little. I'd inherited nothing but memories from my parents, but they were worth more to me than anything. It was too late to be a good daughter to them in life, but by giving them this grave, I'd be able to stay close to them, and they in turn could always be together. I hoped Dad would finally have peace and quiet to read my last letter to him.

Dear Dad,

I always loved you so much. But when I saw you come home drunk with those hostesses on your arm, I couldn't stand it. I was terrified that you would abandon us and run away with those women. And I believed if you went away, then Mom might have to leave us too. Because I was so afraid that would happen, and because I didn't want to make you mad, I did everything to try and stay on your good side when I was little. I didn't want to lose you.

In the end, we lost our house and everything in it, and Mom's dream of buying a new house for us all to live in together never came true. I really wanted to help you out with that, but I couldn't. I couldn't even keep my promise to you not to split up with Taka. I'm sorry for being such an ungrateful daughter. Please forgive me, Dad, for everything. I'm leaving you the talisman you bought me all those years ago. It's the only thing I have left now from when I was little, and it's my most precious possession. I want you to take it to remember me by. I know you'll be watching over us all from heaven. Tell Mom I love her too, OK?

Shoko

On my thirty-third birthday, a parcel arrived from Maki. I untied the red bow and pulled off the wrapping paper. I found a beige cashmere scarf with a letter from Dad. Before he'd died, he'd handed it to Maki with instructions to give it to me once I had settled down and got my life together.

Dear Shoko,

Ever since you were little, you were such a kind and gentle child. You were the one who always looked after our pets. It brings tears to my eyes to think what a good heart you have. I wanted to meet Taka one more time and ask him to be sure to take good care of you, but it looks like I won't have the chance now. In my eyes, you're still as good-hearted as you were as a kid. It's just your health that worries me. Please take extra care of yourself and make sure you don't work too hard. These are probably my last words to you, so Shoko, please continue to believe in yourself.

Dad

It was as if a reply had come back to me from heaven. And at that moment, I realized that I had always subconsciously been looking for my father in the men I'd chosen to love. I finished reading Dad's letter, folded it back up and slipped it back into its white envelope. I decided it was time to quit the hostess business.

Mama-san accepted my month's notice, and I put everything I had into one final spurt. I was just within reach of the number one spot. I was lucky enough to have a regular who was a big-spending lawyer, and thanks to him, I was bringing in big bucks at the club.

My last day of work came right as the cherry blossom was starting to bloom, bringing back all those fond memories. Nearly all my regular clients turned up, and those who couldn't make it sent bouquets. Payday wouldn't be until the tenth of the following month, so I didn't know how I'd done, but I knew I'd worked as hard as I could, and I was left with no regrets. As I was getting ready to leave, I picked up each of the bouquets and read the message cards. It was great to read each client's kind words. There was even one from Taka.

Congratulations on all your hard work. I wish you luck finding your new path in life.

His was the only bouquet that I took home with me.

"Please keep the flowers for the club. I'll just take the cards with me."

"We'd love to, but are sure you don't want to take them?" asked Mama-san.

"No, I'm good. You don't mind keeping them, do you?"

"Yeah, you're right. If you try to get all this home, the taxi's going to look like a florist's delivery van," said one of the guys on the staff. The others all laughed.

"Thank you for everything. It was fun," I said to everyone.

"What's going to be more fun for you is next month's pay packet!" said Mama-san, curling the corners of her scarlet-painted mouth into a smile. Then she asked in her sexy voice, "Since it's your last day, Shoko-chan, shall we go out on the town?"

I politely refused and hailed a cab instead. On the way back to my apartment, I called Taka on my cell phone.

"Thanks for the flowers."

"What are you going to do now?"

"Well, first I'm going to get a day job. Then I'm going to do what I've always wanted to do since I was a kid. I'm going to try to become a writer."

"You, a writer?" Taka started to laugh.

"I thought you'd find it funny. But I'm serious."

"I see. You're not worried about being alone?"

"No."

"If things get tough, don't let it get you down, all right?"

"I won't."

"Take care now."

"Bye, Taka."

I pushed a couple of buttons on my phone, and a message appeared on the screen.

Delete contact?

I pushed *yes*.

Contact deleted.

"Excuse me, you can let me out here."

The taxi driver was surprised. "You sure, lady? We still have a ways to go."

"I feel like walking."

"OK then," he said stopping the meter. "Good night."

I handed him the fare.

"D'you need a receipt?"

"No, I'm fine. Thank you."

I got out and began to walk home, carrying the bouquet.

Meow!

Over the clack of my painfully high heels, I caught the faint mewing of a kitten. I wandered around for a while trying to find the source of the sound.

Meow!

I could still hear the cry, but the kitten was nowhere to be seen. Then I heard a rustling noise. Down in the deep rain gutter at the side of the street was a pile of garbage bags. I found the kitten inside one of them. It was scrawny and caked in mud.

"Poor thing. All alone in a place like this. Hey, so am I. Do you want to come and live with me?"

Meow!

"We'll have to think of a good name for you."

A full moon shone down from the night sky as I hugged the kitten to my chest.

I think a lot about the moon. How it constantly waxes and wanes, just like my life with its highs and lows. I like to think of myself as having been born under a new moon. Then, in those uncertain days when I was searching for love, I guess the moon would have been a crescent. It was probably about a half-moon when I got married. Now that I'm alone, do I warrant a full moon? Have I finally overcome my weaknesses and grown up? I'm heading off along a new path in life, but if it turns out to be a dead end, I guess I can start over with the next new moon.

Whatever happens, wherever I go, this moon will be smiling down at me, its light as soothing to me as my mom's love. It won't do to lie or cheat or fake it this time. There's no way I'm going back to the days I couldn't look my own father in the eye. And someday I'm sure I'm going to meet the one, the person who will care enough about me to make me their number one. I know the moon will be shining extra-brightly that night.

On the tenth, I went over to Mama-san's place to pick up my pay packet.

"Good job. You made number one."

I held out both hands—bare now without their brightly polished nail extensions—and Mama-san dropped the envelope into them. It was heavy, and I felt a great sense of accomplishment, like the first time I rode my bike as a kid.

Mom had stood a short distance away, holding out her hands and calling, "Shoko-chan, come on! Ride to me!"

"Shoko, don't look back, OK? I'm going to hold on back here, and I want you to pedal as hard as you can," Dad instructed me.

The handlebars were wobbling like crazy.

"Keep going! Don't look back. Keep looking straight ahead and pedal. Go on! Harder!"

The bike stopped wobbling and at that moment, Dad let go.

"You're doing it all by yourself!"

I rode like the wind.

Thank you Mom and Dad.

Shoko Tendo, 2004.

Afterword

I began working on this book in 2002. I was single again, trying to find out what my strengths and weaknesses were, and busy imagining a future for myself. It was at this turning point in my life that I made the decision to write my memoirs and look back over the road I'd traveled.

I became a juvenile delinquent at the age of twelve, soon became hooked on amphetamines and sex, and was involved with a string of married men. It was painful for me to revisit this sordid past. But on the other hand, writing about it was very freeing. I rid myself of demons that had been plaguing me, and felt able to smile again for the first time in a long while.

It has taken the support and kindness of many, many people for someone like me, who never really had any education, to fulfill my dream of becoming a writer. Many a time, the words wouldn't flow, and I got discouraged. In the end I realized that what was important in writing an autobiography was not to make myself look good or to create beautiful prose, but to stay true to myself. This is what I learned from the loving letter I received from my father after his death. Still, I fell way behind schedule and I caused a great deal of trouble for everyone involved. I count myself incredibly lucky that so many people gave me their support and helped me to finish the book.

The old me not only abused people physically, but also wounded them deeply with my words. I truly regret what a terrible person I used to be. There's still a lot I don't know about life, but it's my guess that the heartbreak and the joy that love can bring is something that helps us grow.

In the meantime, I'm groping my way in the murky real world, trying to find where I belong. It's not easy to work out where you're supposed to be; even those people whose lives are so-called success stories have gone through their own struggles, although it's not always immediately obvious to others. I'm convinced they got where they are today by believing in themselves.

It's not appearances that are important, but making the best of what you've got inside. I don't care how long it takes, if I can make it by staying true to what I believe in, I'm sure that real happiness is waiting for me. I think the answer to how to live my life has always been inside me, and I just need to put it into practice. I think it's true to say that I haven't done anything momentous or beautiful in my life up till now, and if my life seems shallow to you, I wouldn't argue with that.

There are many things that I wanted to write here but didn't dare to. It's enough for me if you can take what I have been able to record here in writing and interpret it as you will. I'm afraid that it will be difficult for you to overlook how poorly written the book is at times, and I apologize for that. I'd love one day to be the kind of writer with the ability to turn you, the reader, into the main character, to transport you to places you've never been, to describe surroundings so vividly that you feel they're there before your eyes, to make your heart beat faster.

Finally, I would like to thank from the bottom of my heart all those people who helped in the publication of this book: everyone involved in the publishing process, my friends who helped me see what was important, and finally, you the reader, who picked up this book and read it through to the end. Thank you for your support now and in my future projects.

Shoko Tendo

How Full is the Moon?

by Manabu Miyazaki

I didn't want to read *Yakuza Moon*. To be honest, I was afraid of reading it. I thought that all my own bad old memories would resurface. And, of course, it was just as I'd feared. But then I was struck by something else. However cruelly fate treats people, however miserable life can be, there are those who will accept the challenge to plumb the depths of that misery to find the essence of what really lies deep inside themselves. I found that deeply moving.

As I read *Yakuza Moon*, I frequently recognized the same environment I grew up in, and the same experiences I went through. I'd like to write a little about that background.

Sukiyaki with Mom

The importance of the mother figure for children growing up in a yakuza household is slightly different from that of a regular household. The yakuza mom is at the beck and call of a violent husband who does whatever he wants, but to her kids she is the essence of motherhood.

My own mother was born in 1913 and she was a very traditional Japanese woman. This was reflected in the way we ate too. When any of us kids had something special on, for example the night before a big game or an exam, my mother would make sukiyaki for dinner. In other words, she thought that sukiyaki was a special dish. I think she believed that it would give us strength. It seems Shoko Tendo's mother thought the same way.

I have a very painful memory associated with the eating of sukiyaki, however. My yakuza father had a demolition business, which my older brother and I inherited. Unfortunately, due to our sloppy management practices, the business went bankrupt. This was around the beginning of the 1980s, when I was about thirty-five. It's a long story, but due to lots of things that were going on in my life at that time, I had made up my mind to kill myself. The night before I was planning to do it, my mother turned up at the dingy little one-room apartment where I was hiding out from debt collectors. She announced that she was going to make me suki-yaki, and right there in the communal kitchen of that horrible dump, she prepared some rice and cooked up a pot of sukiyaki. She never actually told me not to kill myself. She simply announced with a smile that she'd brought me some luxury Matsuzaka marbled beef. That smile stopped me from committing suicide.

About a year before the bankruptcy problems, my brother and I had been put on the nationwide police wanted list over illegal business prac-tices. When I decided to turn myself in to the police, my mother stayed tough, telling me not to worry what might happen, and above all not to tell the police any more than I needed to. For me there was no difference between the look on her face then, and the time she smiled and told me that she'd brought Matsuzaka beef.

My mother passed away ten years later. At her wake, my older sister, brother, and I were placing her favorite possessions in her coffin for her to take with her, when I noticed her treasured tortoiseshell glasses were missing. My sister knew what had happened to them. It was only as my mother lay in her coffin that I learned that her precious tortoiseshell glasses had been sold to make me Matsuzaka beef sukiyaki ten years earlier. Sukiyaki with Mom is a truly painful memory.

Yakuza Business

As you know, both Shoko Tendo and I come from yakuza families. Her father's businesses started out well and appeared to be successful, but because they were run by a yakuza, they were eventually doomed to fail. And it was pretty much the same case with my father.

Yakuza are by nature both flamboyant and cocky. If they weren't more flamboyant and cocky than the average guy, then they wouldn't become yakuza. But at the same time, simply because they possess these characteristics, they will end up either incredibly successful, or crash and burn spectacularly. Particularly if they are in business, these typical yakuza character traits are often the root of their demise. We can see this most clearly when they are faced with debt.

Because of their position as yakuza, they have easy access to loans. They can amass billions of yen without putting up any kind of collateral, but only as long as the loan is at a super high rate of interest. This is because, among yakuza, the fact that the borrower is a yakuza is enough security. There is no mention of any of the usual bothersome details required by regular financial institutions, such as assets, or a guarantor, or even submitting a business plan. I would go so far as to say a yakuza's own body is his collateral. So yakuza can raise funds with ease. But that's the problem. That's where Shoko Tendo's experience overlaps with my own.

In real life, businesses can't survive on loans with interest rates of 10 percent every ten days. Quite simply, with interest like that to pay, you go bankrupt. But because yakuza are so relentless in their need to show off, and too stubborn to stop when things are going wrong, they resort to taking out these questionable loans. Consequently, their failure ends up being utterly disastrous. When a yakuza goes bankrupt, it is common for a hitherto heroic male to suddenly hole himself up in his house or go on the lam, leaving his wife to swallow her pride and go right out the next day and find herself a job to support her family. I've seen this happen many times. She displays a necessary survival instinct, the very antithesis of her husband's flamboyant and cocky behavior. You could say that the woman who has always stood quietly in the shadow of her macho yakuza man turns out to be the one with true spirit.

Juvenile Delinquency

Shoko Tendo tells us her delinquency began in middle school. Mine was a little later, but it does tend to occur a little earlier with girls than boys. In fact, I've been very interested in this topic of juvenile delinquency for some time. In my case, my turning delinquent was actually an attempt to be more like an adult. If I was an adult, I wouldn't have to go to school anymore; I could go and see movies and hang around downtown without being scolded by my parents. That's why I wanted to grow up quickly. Unfortunately, growing up takes time, and I couldn't wait that long. So my friends and I played at being adults. A group of us who felt the same way got together. And that's how our gang was created.

It's interesting to me now that in our gang whoever did the worst thing was the coolest—that is, they got the respect of the rest of us for being the most "adult." So of course we ended up competing with each other for who could be the "baddest." We didn't even hesitate to move from shoplifting to inhaling paint thinner, from thinner to sleeping pills, and then on to amphetamines. And this all happened in a very short period of time. We believed that speed was much cooler and adult than thinner. Each "step up" was like our own coming-of-age ceremony. That's how kids who had only just begun to stray from the straight and narrow rapidly ended up part of a whole subculture. Even though my gang was very loosely structured, and we did occasionally betray our friends or inform on them to police, it felt comfortable to be a member. There was one important element—we believed we had the kind of solidarity that had been lost in other communities such as school, neighborhood, and even family. The members who sensed this solidarity would stick with the gang, and those who didn't quickly left.

What I found the most interesting and surprising was that communication between gang members was always polite. The boys and girls in the gang treated each other with respect. And that was attractive to kids who were anxious to be adults.

Speed

Tendo has written a lot about her experiences with speed. I acknowledge that speed is a serious problem in today's society. However, for someone like me, surrounded by so many users, I can tell you that lecturing people that using drugs is a crime is pointless. Words have no power over them. The problem is too deep.

Where can I begin to talk about what speed does to people? Hallucinations are a common first symptom. Users become convinced someone is watching them and trying to kill them. I've had regular late night phone calls begging me to go and check out a shadow behind some lamppost. Another user's mother came to me beside herself with worry, thinking her son had gone crazy. She explained that when he went to sleep at night he sprinkled a two-inch-wide rectangle of black pepper around his futon with such careful precision that it looked like he must have used a ruler to measure it. When she asked him if it was some kind of magic spell, he answered in all seriousness that he'd been troubled by bugs crawling all over his body while he slept, and the pepper was to keep them away. When she heard this, his mother was convinced her son had lost his mind. These stories sound like funny anecdotes, but things also go wrong, and these people can end up harming others.

I'd often heard that there is far more of a connection between speed and sex for female users than for male. Reading *Yakuza Moon* was the first time I realized to what extent it was true.

Of course, I know of cases where users have been hospitalized and treated for their addiction, but it seems to me the fastest way to kick the habit is to get arrested and thrown in jail...

Yakuza Neighborhoods

My early childhood interactions with neighbors seem to have been very like Shoko Tendo's. The neighborhoods around yakuza families are usually filled with ill-will, accompanied by a degree of jealousy. Yakuza are outsiders with no chance of enjoying the feeling of being part of a community.

Wherever a yakuza family lives, their non-yakuza neighbors tend to gossip about them, complaining about how they act like big shots with their expensive, imported cars, but how they'll soon get what's coming to them. How they'll be brought down a peg or two when their business fails. Or how once the husband gets thrown in jail, the family will fall apart. And then at school, the kids of the worst gossipmongers repeat what they've heard to the kids of the yakuza families. They've heard their mothers tell these stories and they believe them as fact. Interestingly, the fathers of these households, being a little more knowledgeable about the power of the yakuza, tend to keep their mouths shut for fear of reprisals.

Unfortunately, it often happens that these vicious rumors turn into reality. Many yakuza families live prosperously for a time but end up having to get out of town quickly. Yakuza mothers and kids are burdened with the bad karma of having to live and grow up in a community filled with malice.

I see Shoko Tendo's *Yakuza Moon* as her way of denying who she was. I think she probably hates yakuza. But by finally facing up to these yakuza, and accepting that the person she used to be only existed in the minds of the yakuza men in her life—including her father—she has set out to reinvent herself. That "moon" she saw shining down on the sad events of the first half of her life, I wonder how brightly it is shining for her now?

Manabu Miyazaki is a best-selling Japanese writer, known for his social criticism and for his yakuza ties. His autobiographical work *Toppamono* has sold more than 600,000 copies in Japan, and has been translated into English.

（英文版）極道な月
Yakuza Moon

2007年3月　第1刷発行
2007年9月　第2刷発行

著　者　天藤湘子
訳　者　ルイーズ・ヒール
発行者　富田 充
発行所　講談社インターナショナル株式会社
　　　　〒112-8652 東京都文京区音羽1-17-14
　　　　電話　03-3944-6493（編集部）
　　　　　　　03-3944-6492（マーケティング部・業務部）
　　　　ホームページ　www.kodansha-intl.com

印刷・製本所　大日本印刷株式会社

落丁本・乱丁本は購入書店名を明記のうえ、講談社インターナショナル業務部宛に
お送りください。送料小社負担にてお取替えします。なお、この本についてのお問い
合わせは、編集部宛にお願いいたします。本書の無断複写（コピー）、転載は著作権
法の例外を除き、禁じられています。

定価はカバーに表示してあります。